CONSCIOUS
GOLF

CONSCIOUS
GOLF

THE **THREE SECRETS** OF **SUCCESS** IN **BUSINESS, LIFE** AND **GOLF**

GAY HENDRICKS

RODALE

Printed in the United States of America

Rodale Inc. makes every effort

to use acid-free ∞, recycled paper ☻.

Book design by Susan P. Eugster

Library of Congress Cataloging-in-Publication Data

Hendricks, Gay.
    Conscious golf : the three secrets of success in business, life and
golf / Gay Hendricks.
        p.   cm.
    ISBN 1–57954–693–5   hardcover
    1. Golf—Miscellanea.   2. Success in business.   3. Conduct of life.
I. Title.
GV873.H39   2003
796.352—dc21   2002153809

Distributed to the book trade by St. Martin's Press

2   4   6   8   10   9   7   5   3   1   hardcover

CONTENTS

CHAPTER 1

THREE SECRETS THAT SHOULDN'T BE KEPT

I've never been good at hiding how I feel, so I'll come right out with it:

Golf is the greatest game of all, and golfers are the luckiest people on earth. If you play golf, you are blessed with the rarest of gifts: to walk in beauty, to enjoy fine companionship and to discover the true essence of living with every swing.

What more could we ask of any game?

Embedded in the game is something vast and limitless but also practical. In particular, golf is the perfect arena where you can master the three secrets of success in business and life. By learning the three secrets of conscious golf, you can get better at golf, business and life—all at the same time! In working with nearly a thousand executives over the past 30 years, my colleagues and I have discovered that the master moves of golf, business and life are the exactly the same.

I consider these three master moves the very foundation skills of good golf, good business and good living. If you understand how to apply these skills, you will know how to stride the full round of your life with integrity, zest and good success.

In this book I make clear distinctions between the three master moves primarily for the sake of understanding. In teaching them to several thousand people, I've found that it really helps to break the moves into distinct components. In the early stages of learning to drive a car, it's helpful to practice putting your foot on the brake over and over as a separate skill. Ultimately, though, you steer and accelerate and brake as part of one automatic movement. The same is true for the three secrets of conscious golf. When you're out there in the fast, real world of golf (or business or life), you'll ultimately find that the three moves blur into one. My hope is that the three master moves will become one smooth automatic move, whether you're driving a golf ball or a hard bargain.

THE PERFECT WAY
TO LEARN ABOUT BUSINESS AND LIFE

Golf gives us two gifts at once: Insight and transcendence. We reveal who we are as we play the course—that much is certain. Play a single hole of golf with three strangers and you will have immediate insight into whether you would have dinner with them, do business with them or loan them your car to drive around the block. However, golf gives us a great deal more: With every swing of the club we have the chance to ascend to new heights of the person we wish to become.

I didn't realize all this until I was well into midlife. In fact, I've come full circle in my attitudes about golf. Earlier in my life I thought it was the stupidest game I'd ever seen. I grew up steeped in baseball. My grandfather was the groundskeeper at a minor league ballpark in the area of Florida where most of the big-league teams came for spring training. As a result, I spent a lot of my childhood watching baseball and hanging around ballplayers. To my young mind, baseball was the only game that really mattered.

At a deeper level, I think my initial sour opinion of golf was probably based on sour grapes. Golf looked to me like a game for the "rich kids," and I definitely was not one of those. Also, I often saw boys going off to play golf with their fathers, and I did not have one of those, either. (My father died at the end of World War II, during the time my mother was pregnant with me.) This condition—not rich, no dad—probably caused me to devalue golf so that I wouldn't feel bad about not being able to play.

As for watching golf on television—forget it. Compared to games I liked, such as baseball and football, golf looked about as interesting as a 4-hour session of watching paint dry. Plus, there were those awful checkered pants that the golfers of the 1950s seemed to favor. I figured that any game people played in checkered pants had to be regarded with intrinsic suspicion. I very much enjoy the sweet irony of life's delightful twists, that I should have come from that background to be a cheerleader for the cosmic potential of golf.

BEYOND NEWTON, BEYOND EINSTEIN

The game of golf, like the game of life, changes according to how you observe it. Perhaps you're familiar with the Heisenberg Principle from the world of physics. Werner Heisenberg discovered that the act of looking at certain particles caused them to move differently. I like to think of golf in the same way. Imagine picking up a prism and looking through it down the fairway toward the flag. Turn the prism one way and you see a dozen different images. Turn the prism just right and you might see a rainbow.

Here is the practical application of that idea: Most players do not succeed at golf, business or life because they are playing from a Newtonian mind-set. They are using a Newtonian paradigm in games that have gone far beyond the limited Newtonian view of the world. The Newtonian worldview is still useful today, but only if it is held in a larger context of the Einsteinian breakthrough of 100 years ago. Play Einsteinian golf and you will discover rich treasures never before imagined. The Einsteinian game will allow you to delight yourself with every swing of golf, business or life. Beyond the Einsteinian game, though, there is a third way. And here we discover the true miracles of possibility.

The first two secrets of *Conscious Golf* correspond roughly to the Newtonian and the Einsteinian paradigms, whereas the third secret carries us into a quantum wonderland of infinite (infinitely practical) understanding.

Let me explain.

Sir Isaac Newton saw an orderly universe that worked according to fixed rules—for every action there was an equal and opposite reaction. The roles you live in shape the rules you live by, and we must remember that Newton lived in a time of rigidly fixed roles. Golf began around the time of Sir Isaac, in the class-bound Britain of the 1600s. From a distance the game still looks purely Newtonian. If you had never seen golf played and were watching it from a nearby hillside, you'd conclude the following: Traveling in small bands, people strike balls with sticks, then proceed in a more or less linear fashion to where the balls have come to rest. Then they hit the balls again. This sequence continues until the balls disappear into a hole in the ground. It is a linear operation, governed by the unforgiving but reliable laws of gravity.

This observation would lead you to a Newtonian conclusion: The perfect shot would go into the hole every time—there wouldn't be so many stops and starts along the way. This type of thinking would lead you to build better golf clubs, longer drivers, and straighter putters. The Newtonian paradigm has resulted in many wonderful improvements in golf equipment since Sir Isaac's time. I know, because I'm benefiting from some of them. Today's terrific equipment allows golfers like me (that is, those who are devoid of natural athletic skill) to hit towering drives and sink tricky putts. If yesterday's great players—Bobby Jones, Walter Hagen, Sam Snead—could be reborn to play with the clubs Tiger Woods and Phil Mickelson get to use, I can virtually guarantee that Tiger and Phil would be sweating a lot more on those summer weekends.

So, hats off to Sir Isaac and the millions of hours of work that have been spent since his time tinkering with the physical dimension of the game. It is only when the Newtonian paradigm becomes a fixation that it gets us into trouble.

From the Newtonian view we would say, "There is a perfect golf shot and our job is to hit it." The Newtonian view says, "There is an ideal and we should aim to find it." The trouble with the Newtonian view is that most of the time we don't come anywhere near hitting a perfect shot, leading a perfect life, running a perfect business, finding a perfect love. If we're stuck in the Newtonian trap, we fall constantly into the gap between the ideal and the real. Looking down the fairway with a Newtonian view, we almost always see a gap between the perfect shot and the one we actually hit. When we hit a ball that doesn't go perfectly, we're stuck with only two reactions. If we're in a good mood, we think, "Oh, well." If we're in a bad mood, we say, "Oh, ****." A Newtonian perspective makes us miserable most of the time—in golf, in life, in love. The Newtonian view also dooms us to poor success in business.

If we go into our business day with a Newtonian mind-set, we're likely to have a very bad day. It's great to have high standards for how you want things to be, and it's perfectly fine to hold out for the best in ourselves and others. However, there's a big difference between high standards and fixed expectations. Fixed expectations grow out of fear; high standards grow from vision and commitment. People with high standards have a vision of what's possible and an ongoing commitment to making that vision a reality. When we lock into a Newtonian mind-set—This is the way things have to be!—we do a major disservice to the creative possibilities of the moment. In each moment is the possibility of rich learning and breakthrough invention, but this possibility can bloom into reality only if we let go of fixed expectations. In other words, life only works well when we can move beyond fear to flow. When we're in the flow we can come up with solutions to problems in the fast-moving world of Right Now. When we're ruled by fixed expectations we're limited to applying yesterday's solutions to today's problems.

I remember encountering this problem for the first time in a construction job the summer I graduated from high school. A crew of about fifty of us were building a bridge over a river. It was a brutally hot summer in the jungles of central Florida. We were supervised by a foreman, Mike, who had very rigid ideas about how things had to be. On the fateful day I recall, his Newtonian view clashed mightily with my Einsteinian perspective.

My job was chipping excess concrete off the underside edge of the bridge. The only safe and sane way to do it was to sit on the bridge, dangle my legs over the side and bend over to chip the concrete between my legs. I was making good progress until Mike came along and ordered me to do it from a kneeling or standing position. I looked up and grinned, thinking he was joking with me. One look at his angry face, though, let me know he was serious. I didn't realize that my way of doing the task was violating one of his sacred rules: Never sit down on the job.

I showed him that trying to do it from a standing position was impossible—nobody could reach down under the bridge unless they had 6-foot-long arms and could bend like a pretzel. Doing it from a kneeling position was not only hard on the knees but dangerous. There was a drop of 18 feet to the river. It was the sluggish season and there was only about 3 feet of water in the river—the last guy who'd accidentally tumbled in was fished out with a broken shoulder. I proudly showed Mike my efficient and safe procedure, expecting him to beam with approval or say, "Dang, son, you really on to sumpin'." In reality, though, he got red in the face, spit out his wad of chewing tobacco and roared at me to get up and do what he told me to do. I think his exact words were, "Ain't nobody ever gonna sit down on no job I'm running." He fixed me with a burning glare until I got on my knees and started chipping. He stalked off muttering about "college boys," an epithet that was synonymous in his lexicon with other nonmanly entities such as "pansies," "pinkos" and "mama's boys." Although technically I was not yet a college boy, there was no use arguing this subtle point. I'd made the mistake of telling him when I was hired that I could work only until college started. I'd been branded for life.

I used the "Mike" technique for a half-hour or so, but soon my knees were aching and I was getting tired of teetering on the brink, watching my balance to keep from doing a header into the muddy river. Mike usually came by only every few hours, so I decided to go back to my own technique. Soon I was comfortably chipping away at my former efficient pace—that is, until Mike unexpectedly came back. I was lost in my chipping trance and didn't hear him come up behind me. He made his presence known, though, by simultaneously bellowing and giving me a kick with his big construction boot—right in the part of me he didn't want me to be sitting on. It scared me more than hurt, and I practically levitated about a foot up off the bridge. He proceeded to give me about 15 minutes of torrential verbal abuse, stringing all his favorite epithets together in creative new combinations like "pansie-mammyjammer." Then he fired me. "Get your sorry college ass off my bridge" was the way I think he put it.

It was a textbook clash between the fixed and the fluid, the absolute and the relative, the Newtonian and the Einsteinian. It's a perfect example of the fatal flaw in the Newtonian paradigm: It works great right up until the moment it doesn't work at all. Mike's fixed view of the world was governed by an ironclad proverb: Never sit down on the job. "Sitting down on the job" was an affront to a moral rule that must be obeyed at all costs, even if it made the job longer, harder and more dangerous.

I trudged off the bridge, taking my Einsteinian pride and my unapologetic rump off to my college-boy destiny. I hitchhiked a ride toward my home 12 miles away, and on the way I tasted the sweetly ironic end to the story. Spotting my mother's car in the parking lot of a radio station, I asked the driver to stop and let me off so that I could get a ride home with her. While waiting for her to finish her business, I struck up a conversation with the station manager, who ended up offering me a part-time job as a disc jockey. I spent the rest of the summer making higher wages than at my construction job, earning every dollar of it sitting down on the job.

THE EINSTEINIAN GAME

If Newton's worldview was too fixed, Einstein's sometimes seems too relative to get a fix on. Once you understand what he was getting at, though, both your golf game and your life game will change greatly for the better.

Einstein described a different universe and a different role for us in it. Remember Einstein's example: An hour with your beloved seems like a minute, whereas a minute sitting on a hot stove feels like an hour. In other words, the way we see reality can change in the wink of an eye, depending on whether we are expanding into the experience of the moment or contracting away from it! The truly exciting Einsteinian idea is this: How we *be* in the universe affects how we experience reality. This is directly opposite from how Newton saw it. In his world, it's how the *universe* is that affects how we are. Period, over and out.

Einstein's view is a great deal more empowering. If you go into your business day with a Newtonian mindset, you run the risk of disempowering yourself with every interaction. If you feel angry, for example, you'll be tempted to think, "Joe didn't get the paperwork to me on time; therefore I'm angry." You draw a straight line from Joe to your anger, with the starting point being Joe's action. For every action there's an equal and opposite reaction, says Newton, and it's tempting to see the world in such simple terms. It's a fatal temptation, though, because that's not how the real world operates.

In the real world, thinking that your anger is caused by other people is not only disempowering but dangerous. Both your health and the health of others can be affected for the worse by mislocation of your emotions. If you give other people power over your emotions, you put them in control of your anger, your sadness, your fear and your joy. If you correctly locate your emotions and the responsibility for them in yourself, you take back that power and, with it, the control over your life.

Joe, in fact, may have nothing at all to do with your anger. You may have carried it into the situation from something that happened yesterday or 40 years ago, and Joe just happened to do something that made it look like he caused it. I've seen executives' lives change right before my eyes by their understanding this point. Let me give an example of one such moment that certainly changed a life and may also have saved it. Although it involved only one executive, the ripple effect spread across an entire corporate culture.

I was doing my first coaching session with the number two man at one of the largest computer manufacturers. The CEO wanted me to work with Max on his tendency to get red in the face and yell at people when angry. Although Max could blow up and get over it quickly, people on the receiving end of his blowups often took weeks to recover. I worked with Max on a recent blowup with the number three guy, Bill.

First, I asked Max what had caused his anger. As I suspected he would, he mislocated the source of it. Here's how our conversation went.

MAX: *He didn't bring the data to the meeting with him.*

ME: *So his failure to bring the data to the meeting triggered your anger.*

MAX: *Right.*

Max's view of the situation was purely Newtonian—in walked Bill; POP! went Max. I immediately knew what needed fixing.

ME: *Would you be willing to make a big leap in your understanding of your anger? One that could possibly be very useful to you and helpful to the company?*

MAX: *Sure.*

This interchange was crucial. Without Max's permission and agreement, I would have had no leverage with which to help him. With his agreement and willingness to "make a leap," he now planted his feet firmly in a commitment to change.

I could now make my big move to free him from the Newtonian trap that kept the problem from having been solved a long time ago.

ME: *Max, I notice that when you talk about your anger toward Bill, you clear your throat repeatedly. You also spontaneously touch your hand to your chest.*

MAX: *I didn't notice that. What's that supposed to mean?*

To Max's great credit, he didn't get defensive when I called his attention to these behaviors. That's probably how he got to be worth several hundred million dollars. He'd rather learn than be right.

ME: *It's not an exact science, but in general, body language will help you get to your real emotions. Sadness is the emotion that most people feel in their throat and chest. Most people experience their anger in their jaws and neck and back. Have you ever noticed the fur stand up on the back of a cat or dog when it's angry?*

MAX: *Yes.*

ME: *We're wired the same way. But even though you were talking about anger, your body signaled that something was going on in the sadness zone. If you'd touched your stomach, I would have suggested fear. Most people feel their fear there—butterflies in the stomach and that sort of thing.*

MAX: *Hmmm. So maybe I'm actually sad?*

ME: *Check it out inside yourself. What might you be sad about with regard to Bill?*

MAX: *I'm disappointed in him. He lets me down over and over.*

When he said the last sentence, his voice changed pitch, dropping to a lower register and a softer tone. This shift told me he was talking about something from the past, not just the present situation with Bill.

ME: *And when you scan back through time, what else does that remind you of?*

MAX: *My stepson. I've had the same feeling about him a hundred times.*

ME: *Anybody else?*

MAX (CHUCKLING RUEFULLY): *Myself.*

ME: *You feel sad about times you've let yourself down.*

MAX: *Constantly.*

ME: *Let's pause a moment while you give yourself some room to feel the sadness about all that, rather than just the anger.*

We went further over the next couple of hours, but these interchanges began the healing process for Max. It had a profound impact on his relationships within the top echelon of executives. Rather than pinning his anger on other people, Max began to realize that he brought it into every meeting with him and that the anger was actually fed by a wellspring of old grief. To his great credit, he talked about these realizations openly in an executive meeting. He told them that he popped off in anger because he didn't yet know how to communicate about deeper issues like disappointment and sadness. He asked them to help him by not taking his anger personally.

Although I never used the terms *Newtonian* or *Einsteinian* with Max, his shift was a classic example of a shift from the old paradigm to the new. Seeing through Newtonian eyes, Max thought the problem was simple: Bill makes Max mad. Through Bill's eyes the problem was equally simple: Max scares the hell out of Bill. The paradigm lay at the heart of the problem; the situation not only didn't change as long as they were using a Newtonian mind-set, it couldn't. There's no room in the paradigm for it. The change came about through Max's willingness to stop drawing a linear path from Bill's behavior to Max's anger.

Fortunately Max had the courage to go deeper. He went Einsteinian, and everything changed.

Newtonian golfers think it's their practice and their equipment that determine how they hit the ball. Einsteinian golfers certainly acknowledge the importance of practice and good equipment, but they know that how you are inside plays an even greater role in how you hit the ball. This insight is profoundly challenging to many of us—it suggests that we succeed by awareness and self-examination. People who love the Einsteinian approach agree with Ralph Waldo Emerson that the unexamined life is not worth living. However, many others lock into the Newtonian game and don't let go. They mock the Einsteinian player as overly mystical. Newtonian golfers prefer to focus on the physical aspects of the game. The makers of golf equipment dearly love Newtonians, though—they'll buy every new thing that comes along.

It works the same way in business. The Newtonian businessperson sets goals, monitors expenses, keeps an eye on the competition. Einsteinian businesspeople do those things, too, but they know that how we are inside is the real determinant of success in business. They've seen the seemingly miraculous twists of timing that come from shifting their inner points of view. One moment things will be sluggish, difficult, blocked. Then, an inner shift brings about a sudden state of insight and clarity. As if by magic, things begin to flow on the outside, too. Funds become available, a permit gets approved, a stock takes off. The Newtonian businessperson must rely on hard work and long hours to get to the goal. The Einsteinian works smart, not hard, and takes exactly the time required to achieve the goal.

THE THIRD WAY

There is a third way to play the game, but we can only gain access to it by progressing through the Newtonian and Einsteinian stages of our development. The third way unlocks golf's true mysteries and ultimate subtleties. The third way can take us all the way to the ultimate golf shot and the ultimate secrets of life on our splendid planet. The third way makes every moment of life a genuine hoot, an eternal whirl with the cosmos itself as our dancing partner.

The third way is about relationships.

It's about our relationship with the ball, and it's about a great deal more.

It's about our relationship with the universe around us, including our companions on the journey. Yet it's about a great deal more.

It's about those moments in life and love and business and golf when the boundaries disappear and we are one with the activity at hand.

It's about graceful leaps out of time. In those exalted moments you don't remember your swing or your striking of the ball—but somehow the ball appears in flight against the spacious sky. In those moments you don't see or hear your companions—but somehow you feel their camaraderie and the resulting richness of your life. In those moments you know you live on earth—but you feel the promise of an eternal home beyond the stars.

In those moments there is no such thing as a bad golf shot. Every shot we hit goes exactly where it is supposed to go, given how it is hit. Whether our shots are "bad" or "good" is merely a made-up concept we've invented to keep from having fun all the time. If we are sufficiently open to learning, we can learn from every shot, every moment of life. In business, we can learn something from every which way the deal goes.

I have never come up with a catchy name for this third way. I really wish I could name it after a physicist so that it would be consistent with Newton and Einstein. Unfortunately I haven't found one yet. For the time being we'll just call it the Third Way. I believe that the Third Way can take us to a saner world. In the new, saner world I envision, the flow of relationship means more to us than anything else.

A SANER WORLD

None of the secrets in this book should be a secret at all. In a saner world, we would start learning these simple things in kindergarten, then practice them every day on the course, throughout the span of our lives. (As I'm sure you'll agree, all elementary schools should provide at least a nine-hole course for the students. High schools, of course, should have a full 18-hole course on the grounds. If budgetary considerations are a factor, I recommend doing away with the social studies faculty.)

In my ideal educational system, we'd begin the day with a golf lesson, then spend the rest of the day honing our ability to live according to the larger principles. We'd study the secrets, spend an hour chipping and putting, then move on to subjects of less significance, such as reading, math and social studies. Then, school would let out after lunch so that the students could get in a full round before dark.

I remember spending hours memorizing those state capitals, especially the tricky ones. I've been lugging this information around for more than 4 decades now, and not once has anyone come up and asked, "Gay, do you happen to know the capital of Montana or South Dakota?" I've been poised for years to blurt out "HELENA!" and "PIERRE!" but so far I haven't had occasion to spout forth my long-stored wisdom. By contrast, there are thousands of times I could have benefited from a little more golf practice.

Golf may also be the key to our burgeoning prison population. If you compare the residents of a penitentiary to the membership of a country club, you would find numerous similarities but one striking difference. The level of actual criminal activity would probably be very similar, except that the net value of the country clubbers' crimes would likely be larger. There might be other subtle differences, such as the number of tattoos per capita, but I can virtually guarantee that there would be one major difference between the two groups: golfing ability. I predict there would be a significant lack of golf skill among the inmates of the penitentiary. Simply put, incarcerated prisoners have higher handicaps! This fact raises a key question: Could it be that their entire life trajectory could have been changed for the better by more time on the golf course? We'll never know, but the nice thing about golf is that it's never too late to begin. My solution would be some sort of golfing Peace Corps, a program by which country club members would be required to spend a certain amount of time each year coaching at prison golf courses.

But wait—perhaps I'm getting carried away.

Let's get back to the subject at hand, the secrets.

There are three.

Each one tells us how to hit a superb golf shot.

Each one tells us how to live a superb life.

Each one shines a beam of light on a different facet of the game.

You need to know these secrets—to play better golf, to lead a better life, to be a better businessperson and, yes, to stay out of jail.

Let us begin.

> "MAKE EVERYTHING
> AS SIMPLE AS POSSIBLE,
> BUT NOT SIMPLER."
>
> —ALBERT EINSTEIN

26

CHAPTER 2

THE FIRST SECRET

I want to tell you the First Secret of hitting a superb golf shot. I guarantee you will hit a better shot once you understand the secret. But that's only a small part of its power. The secret has huge implications for the way we live our lives and conduct our business. Once you understand the First Secret, you'll have an extraordinary power in your hands. I've taught it to thousands of people, and I've never had a single person come back and tell me it didn't work. It's that powerful.

I plan to spend about half of this book working with you on the First Secret. If you understand it deeply—heart and soul, belly and bone—you will find the Second and Third Secrets exquisitely sensible and easy to learn.

Let me tell you about the breakthrough moment of discovery that changed my life.

Until that magic day, I had just about everything I wanted, except that I couldn't seem to hit a good, consistent golf shot. That one little thing had been bugging me for years.

I've been richly blessed in just about every other way. My wife, Katie, and I have enjoyed more than 20 years of a great marriage. I made enough money by my fifties so that I no longer had to work unless I wanted to. In addition, my kids were grown and I had plenty of interesting projects in my church and community. From just about every angle, it looked like I had it made—but I couldn't hit a golf ball with satisfying consistency.

Some people would call that a trivial problem. I might even agree with them, but it still bugged me.

I'd had lessons up the kazoo. I had good equipment, and I'd even been suckered into buying a few of those "incredible, new, life-changing" golf products on the infomercials. Believe it or not, I even purchased my Infiniti Q45 partly because it came with a set of Big Bertha clubs as an incentive. Even with a great set of clubs, though, I didn't make appreciable improvement as a golfer.

I had plenty of things to blame it on. For one thing, I'm definitely not a natural athlete. As a kid, I was usually the last one picked for the team, regardless of which sport was popular in the neighborhood. Another problem was that my left eye had 20/20 vision and my right eye 20/80. This difference made my depth perception a little wacky. I had a hard time telling where the ball stopped and the ground started, a problem that caused me to carve out embarrassingly large chunks of real estate from time to time. (I recently had LASIK correction on my right eye, and I'm hitting the ball better as a result.)

Golf is one of those things, like skiing, that I wish I'd started when I was a kid. However, I didn't start playing until I was in my forties. It's also a game that calls for consistent practice, and I don't get out to play more than once a week or so.

So, there was plenty to blame my golf problems on. But, as you've probably discovered, there's not much satisfaction in just having something to blame. It's certainly no match for the exhilaration of success. I wanted to be able to hit a golf ball well, but nothing I tried made it happen.

THE BREAKTHROUGH

Then the magic happened. . . .

I had a flash of insight—one of those split-second

realizations that change everything. One weekend morning, I was hitting balls alone on a driving range when I discovered the First Secret. I'd hit about ten balls with my driver, and none of them had gone where I wanted them to go. Then I topped a ball and hit a grounder, one of those awful "worm burners" that make you sneak a quick look around to see if anybody's watching. I paused for a moment and wondered, "What is it I'm doing wrong? Am I missing something here?" Suddenly the world seemed to stop—everything became still and silent. As easefully as a feather floating down through the air, an insight descended into my mind.

In that moment of insight, I realized there was something I always did that made me successful in the rest of my life, but I *didn't* do it when I tried to hit a golf ball. There was a crucial principle I practiced scrupulously in business, marriage and child rearing—but I didn't practice it when I hit a golf ball.

I suddenly realized that if I didn't do it in golf, there was no reason to expect success. No wonder I hadn't been successful!

Before I had the insight, I had hit about ten balls out of a bucket of fifty, and I'd sprayed them all over the place. After I realized the First Secret, *I hit forty solid shots in a row*. It didn't matter which club I picked up—I hit one satisfying, straight shot after another.

It's been that way ever since. My scores have dropped by a dozen strokes. I'm not ready to run out and join the Senior Tour by any means, but I'm sure playing better than I ever dreamed. It's not because I'm playing more, either. I still play about once a week on the average. But the difference is awesome! One thing, of course, is the pleasure of turning in a scorecard with a lower number on it. That's great, and I'm proud of it. But the real miracle to me is the fun I have now. I always had a good time playing golf, but I felt a lot of frustration, too. Now, the frustration is gone—it's just pure pleasure.

The nice thing about the First Secret is that you can apply it to every area of your life. I'll show you how to hit a golf ball better than you've probably ever done before, but I'll also show you how to be more successful at business and at life itself. The same secret applies across the board.

There's a story about a scholar who goes to visit a Zen master to ask the secret of Zen. The scholar prattles on about how many books he's read, how many articles he's written, how long he's studied and so forth. Finally, the Zen master asks the scholar if he'd like a cup of tea. The scholar says "Yes," but when the master pours the man his cup of tea, he continues to pour after the cup is full. With tea running all over the place, the scholar angrily says, "What are you doing? Can't you see the cup is full?" The Zen master says, "That's why I can't teach you about Zen. Your cup is already so full you don't need any more concepts. Empty your cup and maybe you'll learn something."

In that spirit, let's empty our cups and learn the First Secret.

If possible, I want you to pick up a golf club right now and hold it in your hands. It doesn't matter if you're in your living room, on the course, on a driving range or wherever. I want you to be holding a club for a moment if you possibly can.

Have one in your hands? Okay, I'll trust that you do.

For now, I'd like you to let go of all the advice you've ever gotten about golf. Let go of every concept and every piece of wisdom in every book you've ever read. Set aside all of it for right now. You can always go back and pick it up again, but I want you to come to the First Secret with an open, free, uncluttered mind. It's important.

If you've ever heard the advice of visualizing where you want the ball to go, forget it. It's not wrong or bad or good advice—it's just something you may have heard before. So put it out of your mind for now.

If you've ever heard "Keep your eye on the ball" or "Don't pull your head up," forget all that. Put it out of your mind.

If you've ever been taught the "perfect" grip, forget it for now. Once you learn the First Secret, you can use a baseball grip or a standard golf grip, or you can make up your own—and you'll hit a fine shot, anyway.

If you think one type of club is better than another, forget all that. If you learn the First Secret, you could grope around blindfolded in a golf shop until you find a club, then go right out and hit good shots with it.

Forget it all for now. Put it aside—you can always come back to it later if you want to.

To symbolize letting go of all those things, I'd like you to hold out your club right now and drop it.

Drop the club to symbolize emptying your mind. Get ready for something new. If you're holding only an imaginary club, drop your imaginary club and get ready for something brand-new.

When you're ready to learn the First Secret, reach down and pick up your club. If you possibly can, I want you to be holding a club in your hands when you learn the secret.

Got it in your hands? Okay, I'll trust that you do.

Imagine that you're about to hit a golf ball off a tee with your driver. In the distance you can see the flag marking the hole where you want the ball eventually to come to rest. Now, holding your club in your grip, imagine looking down at the ball.

Address your imaginary ball on your imaginary tee, and prepare to swing your real club at the imaginary ball. In a moment I'll want you to take a slow-motion swing at your imaginary ball.

Focus on the imaginary ball keenly as you take a slow-motion backswing. Now, begin your forward swing toward the ball. You're still eyeing the ball keenly as your club face approaches the ball. Now, the club hits the imaginary ball, which is no longer on the tee.

When you begin your swing, you would naturally want to be focusing on the ball, right? Of course. Your eyes would be watching the ball keenly, or so we would hope.

As you swing the club toward the ball, just before you hit it, you would still want your focus to be on the ball, right? Of course you would. If your focus wanders at this crucial moment, you're in trouble.

But where should you be looking just after you hit the ball? For a split second, you should still be looking at the top of the tee your ball was just sitting on. The ball is no longer there, but if you want to be really sure you've finished the job, you still want to be looking at the tee—where the ball used to be until a split second ago. Only this way can you be sure you have completed the essential task: hitting the ball. Only by keeping your focus on the ball until it's gone can you be sure you haven't abandoned the crucial task—striking the ball—so that you can peek ahead at the outcome. The First Secret cures you of the biggest problem in golf: shifting your attention before you've hit the ball.

Until you hit the ball, no other business matters. The moment after you hit it, it is none of your business anymore. It's going to go where it's going to go, and you have no control over it whatsoever.

Great golfers and great businesspeople give their full attention to the thing that matters most until they know it's been done. After that they let go and put their attention on the next thing that matters most. The only way to know that the ball has departed is to be looking where it was but isn't anymore. Then you can take a look to see how you did.

The First Secret is this: Keep your attention on the essential process until it's complete. Finish the job before you start thinking about the outcome. The secret says: Make sure you've completed one thing before you move on to the next.

The First Secret cures you of a big problem in the rest of your life, too. For many people, the biggest problem they need to fix is the habit of letting their attention wander from essential tasks before completing them. I once had a roomful of fifty people at a seminar make lists of all the things they had "not-quite-finished." We generated hundreds of items, some going back decades. Imagine the amount of energy that gets frittered away by leaving things "not-quite-finished"! It was remarkable how much of a buzz this activity generated—just naming the items freed up a huge amount of pent-up energy.

The First Secret says: Complete the one thing that most needs to be completed before you move on.

Finish one essential process before moving on to the next essential process. The essential process is the thing that must be done—the action that must be taken before other actions become relevant.

Until your ball is no longer on the tee, you have only one essential process that matters, and that is striking the ball. After the ball has left the tee, the next essential process is finding out where you hit it. Many people leave the essential process behind before it's complete. They jerk their heads up to see where the ball went before they've finished hitting it. If you shift your attention to "How'd I do?" before you've finished the job, you'll have trouble—on and off the course.

The First Secret tells us something important about golf, but it gives us crucial advice about business and life. In business, you have to master the skill of completing essential actions. In particular, you have to focus on completing an essential action before you focus on the outcome. If you want one powerful question to focus on throughout the business day, I recommend this one: Did I complete the essential task impeccably? In every situation of golf and business and life, ask yourself, "Did I do everything I could to complete the task impeccably before I went on to the next thing?" If the answer is yes, your outcome is likely to be just fine; however, if the outcome doesn't please you, you will know that you did what you could.

Tom Boyer, the CEO of our Academy for Conscious Golf and Conscious Business, has worked on-site with hundreds of executives and their businesses. His conclusion: "Almost all difficulties I see in the business world come from unclear, incomplete, broken or genuinely unfair agreements." In other words, difficulties come from incompletion.

Here's an example of an unclear agreement:

ME: Let's have lunch tomorrow.

YOU: Great! See you then.

It's pretty obvious what's missing from our conversation: exactly when and where we're going to meet. We agreed to have lunch—that part of our conversation was complete. However, we overlooked the essential next action. I cannot count the number of times I've seen conflicts occur in the business world by lack of clarity in agreements.

All of Tom's examples involve completion or the lack of it. If an agreement is not clear to everyone, it simply means that it was communicated incompletely. If an agreement is broken, it means that one or more people did not complete it. If an agreement is genuinely unfair, it means that there was incompletion in the consideration of all parties. (Slavery is an example of an unfair agreement—all parties were not given a chance to make the agreement by informed consent.)

I believe it was Woody Allen who said that 80 percent of success is "just showing up." He was on the right track, but I think he got his number too low. It's probably closer to 100 percent. Look at Coca-Cola. Are the company's products that much better than whoever is in last place in the soft-drink business? Probably not, but the folks at Coca-Cola certainly know how to show up. They've been showing up for the better part of 100 years. And they show up all over the place, too. Years ago, while trekking in the Himalayas, I paused to rest and admire the view. It had been hours since I'd seen another human being. Suddenly a voice called out, "Hello, Mister." A tiny lady emerged from a cave and waved to me.

I thought perhaps she needed help, but it turned out

she was an entrepreneur. There, inside the mouth of the cave, was her "store." The only decor was a small wooden crate turned upside down to serve as a counter, and on that counter stood her complete inventory: two bottles of pop, both made by Coca-Cola. That, friends, is showing up.

In truth, almost all of success is about showing up. Showing up means many things: getting there on time, following through with what you said you'd do, keeping your promises. Some of the most gifted and talented people I've known in my life failed to achieve success and happiness because they didn't show up reliably.

There's something else important about showing up—it's often the only thing we have control of. Although we do have control of whether we act with integrity, there's no guarantee we'll get rewarded with integrity from the other side. We also have control over whether we speak the truth impeccably, but there's certainly no guarantee people will greet that truth with appreciation or mutual honesty.

The outcome of our actions can rarely be controlled. Nowhere is this fact more maddeningly clear than on the golf course. Even if you hit a beautiful boomer of a drive, a big hungry bird with a twisted sense of humor might swoop down and pluck your ball out of the air. I once saw a magnificent drive (fortunately not my own) fly 300 yards down the fairway, only to disappear into a freshly made gopher hole. In golf, the shot almost never lands exactly where we want it to. It's the unpredictability that makes golf, business and life so fascinating. All we can do is make our part of the game impeccable.

THE PRACTICAL MYSTIC

Let me don two hats at once: Mr. Absolutely Practical and Mr. Utterly Mystical. Let me explain the First Secret in terms that are so practical you can use them at work today and so mystical you can contemplate them for an eternity. Throughout your swing, stay focused on the ball, and keep focusing on it until it isn't there anymore. There's only one way to be sure you haven't jumped ahead with your attention: For a split second, you should still be watching where the ball used to be after it's not there anymore. If you're hitting off a tee, you should be looking at the top of the tee after the ball's gone. If you're hitting off the grass, you should be watching the place on the grass where the ball was until a split second ago.

The secret: Watch the ball until it's not there anymore.

Stay focused on the most essential goal—connecting with the ball—until you're absolutely sure you've completed it impeccably. The only way to measure your success is with your own eyes. If your eyes are looking at where the ball used to be, you've succeeded. Then, and only then, is it time to move on to your next goal.

THE NEXT ESSENTIAL ACTION

In golf, the next goal after hitting the ball is locating the ball. Seeing where the shot went is essential. How we *feel* about where the shot went is not essential. Although many people invoke the name of God just after they hit the ball (and often not in reverent tones), I can virtually guarantee that the Deity doesn't really care where our shots go. The Deity has already done the essential divine task of creating us and the ground under our feet and the clouds above our heads. In addition, He or She has left us with an eternal gift that makes it easier to locate the ball. It's called gravity, and without its Eternal Suck, our balls would be much harder to locate. Without gravity, our heads would be even farther up in the clouds than they already are, and Lord only knows where our balls would be.

The first and biggest fundamental mistake in golf is peeking to see where your shot went before you've completed hitting it. The biggest fundamental mistake in life is failing to finish one thing impeccably before going on to another or paying attention to the outcome. It doesn't matter whether we're doing something seemingly trivial or seemingly important—the same secret applies across the board. People walk away from conversations before they're complete—and this incompletion invariably costs them something later. People walk away from projects large and small—from soups to symphonies—before they've finished. Invariably someone pays the price for leaving projects undone. We walk away from relationships before we've finished the job, only to change partners and repeat the same old patterns all over again.

Until you actually strike the ball, there is no other important goal. The target is just a distant hole in the ground. Ultimately, that hole in the ground will become important, but until you hit the ball, the only goal that matters is making clean contact.

THE DIFFERENCE BETWEEN EXPECTATION AND CONSCIOUS VISUALIZATION

Expectation is one of the biggest obstacles facing the conscious golfer and the conscious businessperson. Most of us come into situations with expectations hovering in the background, and these expectations keep us from being fully in the present. In my work with business executives, I've found that expectations are responsible for many missed opportunities and failed goals. The reason is that expectations are rooted in fear and based on past experiences. If we knew that, we wouldn't have so much trouble with expectations. However, expectations are almost always unconscious.

Let me give an example. I once was helping a three-member executive team work out some communication problems that were hindering a project. We'd made substantial progress in our two previous meetings, but the third meeting veered into the disaster zone before I could figure out what the problem was. When I came into the conference room for our third meeting, I found that the table we usually met around had been removed to have a leg repaired. I didn't think anything of it, so I simply set up four chairs in a circle and got ready for the meeting. The first two executives entered, sat down and started exchanging small talk. One of them mentioned the missing table, and I repeated the information I'd been given (by a secretary) that the table was under repair. They went back to small talk, which continued until the third man, George, entered.

We got underway, but from the very beginning George seemed hostile, withdrawn and out of sorts. Within minutes the mood in the room was worse than it was in our first meeting, and they were wrangling about issues we'd already resolved. After an unpleasant half hour I blew the whistle and tried to get to the bottom of this flare-up of tension. To make a long and sweaty story short, the problem was an expectation of George's, rooted in fear and based on past experience. It emerged that a former consultant had insisted that everyone sit in a circle of chairs for what George scornfully called encounter groups. George hated the forced revelation of feelings the consultant was trying to engineer, and it left a bad taste in his mouth that came back when he entered the room for our meeting.

Immediately upon seeing the circle of chairs, he figured I had removed the table and was going to force them into "encounter" mode. His emotions took over and sabotaged the good mood we'd created in the past two meetings. The remarkable part is that he had no idea of the expectations and fears that were running his behavior until we spent an hour or so digging into why our progress had ground to a halt.

There's a big difference between expectation and visualization. Expectation is usually unconscious, based on the past and rooted in fear. When you approach the ball on the tee, you might have an expectation you're not going to hit a good shot. Perhaps you've just hit a bad one and haven't been able to shake the fear that you're going to do it again. That's very different from a conscious visualization of how you'd like the shot to go. Many golfers like to visualize the kind of shot they'd like to hit, and although I'm not a big fan of that technique, I've seen many golfers who swear by it.

My basic beef with visualization is that it's just one more thing that potentially keeps you from focusing on the First Secret. My philosophical beef with it is that it can keep you out of the present and limit the fully expanded possibilities of the resulting shot. I have found, through hard-won experience, that my chances of making a brilliant shot are best when I focus all my attention on making clean contact and staying with that contact until the ball is no longer there. Anything else I do—visualization included—is a potential barrier to being right with the ball until it's gone.

TO LIFE

Let's apply the same principle to life: While you're doing any activity, stay focused on it until you complete it. Then go on to the next thing. That piece of advice will change your life for the better, and I heartily advise you to practice it.

The same principle applies to every conversation. If we walk away from a conversation before it's complete, we'll pay for that incompletion later. Let me give you an example that has several levels of incompletion in it. Suppose I owe you $100, and you've been wondering when you are going to get it back. We made the classic mistake of not specifying a date by which the money would be paid. One day we meet on the street and stop to chat. If I don't pay you, and if you walk away from that conversation without asking me about the money, you leave incompletion hovering in the air. If you're smart, you'll say, "What's happening with the $100?" Then, we talk about it until we come to completion.

How would we do that?

The easiest way is that I could pay you on the spot. If I do that, we're complete, at least on the purely physical level of reality. Each of us may have feelings about the situation, and we won't be complete on the emotional level until we speak those feelings to each other clearly. You might need to say, "I'm angry that you took so long" or "I'm disappointed in you" or "Take my number out of your Rolodex." I might need to say, "I apologize for letting you down" or "I feel ashamed I didn't pay you back." Emotions usually remain incomplete until we open our mouths and speak them clearly to the significant person.

If I don't pay you on the spot, another way we could get completion is by making an agreement about when I will pay you back. If I commit to paying you back by Friday at midnight, then we're complete for now. Ultimately it depends on what happens by Friday at midnight, but for now, we can both walk away relaxed.

Or you might say, "I forgive the debt." If I go along with that and let you forgive it, then we're complete.

In the course of my consulting work in corporations, I've had the opportunity to spend countless hours in the company of executives. In the initial stages of my work with an executive, I often spend a morning doing something I call shadowing. I simply follow him or her around for a few hours, seeing what I see. I don't speak, unless it's a quick introduction to someone he or she is talking to. On one vivid occasion, I shadowed the CEO for a couple of hours, then did the same thing with the president and the vice president.

I was keeping track of completions. In other words, I was monitoring how many things (including calls, conversations and other communications) were completed impeccably, versus how many left an element of incompletion that needed to get handled later.

When I finished tallying up the scores, here's what it looked like:

CEO: zero incompletions

President: four

Vice president: fourteen

Do you spot a trend there?

From the perspective of coaching a thousand or so executives in the past 3 decades, I can give you a clear answer to that question. The higher you look in an organization, the more you'll see people who complete things impeccably. In the example above, the CEO handled a great many more items than the president, but he did them as gracefully and impeccably as a ballet dancer or matador.

He simply didn't leave loose ends. A call came in from a big Wall Street player, relaying information about what sounded like a huge problem to me. The CEO made a decision, gave an instruction, hung up and sent a group e-mail to the people who needed to know. Then he moved on to a totally different activity, which happened to be a decision about a retirement gift for a person in the shipping and receiving department. It was clear to me that the latter item was getting exactly the same quality of attention as the Wall Street situation. By contrast, while shadowing the vice president, I noticed that he had to make several extra calls to people he'd already talked to, just to handle things he'd forgotten on the original call.

Worry-thoughts are a direct symptom of incompletion. When I wake up in the middle of the night with worry-thoughts buzzing through my mind, the source of those worries is usually incompletion. I've even gone to the trouble of documenting the kinds of incompletions that produce my worry-thoughts, both the daytime and the nightime variety. My number one category:

Things I Said I'd Do and Didn't Get Around To. Even though I've learned to be a consummate maker of "to do" lists, I often manage to leave something significant off the list. Some part of me is busy keeping score, though, because around 3 A.M. my inner referee blows a whistle and I come awake thinking about it. I've learned to keep a pad and pen beside my bed so I can jot down my thoughts and get back to sleep.

IT'S ABOUT ENERGY, NOT MORALITY

The First Secret is about completion and energy. It is not—repeat not—about morality. It doesn't matter whether completion is morally superior to incompletion. The big problem with incompletion is that it saps energy. The big secret about completion is that it frees up energy. Completing one thing impeccably frees up creative energy you can then use for the next thing.

It has been my great pleasure to spend time in the presence of masterful businesspeople such as Michael Dell. It's also been my pleasure to watch carefully as magnificent golfers like Phil Mickelson and Tiger Woods hit balls. I also had the humbling experience of comparing my swing to Tiger's on frame-by-frame video. I mention Michael, Phil and Tiger together because I learned the same thing from watching them in action: They are all masters of energy. Each of these remarkable young men uses his energy in a way that delivers maximum impact.

As of the last time I talked to him, Michael has absolutely no interest in golf. I doubt that Phil or Tiger has any interest in running a company with thirty thousand employees. Yet they all deliver maximum energy at impact. Michael is famous for never engaging in small talk. Nobody told me this before meeting him, so I learned it by awkward experience. We first met in the hall near his office, and after introducing myself, I said something about the scorching July day outside. He looked a little puzzled and said, "Well, we're indoors." There was no trace of sarcasm or unpleasantness—I think he was genuinely puzzled about why a person standing in the coolness of the hall would talk about heat somewhere else! I've since watched with amusement as various people have tried to converse with him about the weather or a big sporting event such as the Super Bowl. He smiles politely and shifts the conversation to something essential. When he speaks, though, you can guarantee that it's worth paying close attention to.

In the video comparison of my swing to Tiger's, it was as plain as day why he hits the ball with such power and precision. There is no wasted energy at the crucial juncture points of the swing! All the energy gets to the ball. Further, there is no "small talk" at each of those juncture points. A wobble in the wrist or an extra maneuver at the top of the backswing is the golf equivalent of small talk. Such unnecessary movements waste time and energy, and they do not advance progress toward the desired goal. Next time you get to watch Phil or Tiger hit a ball, watch their wrists, elbows, shoulders and knees. You won't see those body parts engaging in any small talk. There are no unnecessary micromovements; everything works together in one sweetly harmonious whole. Comparing my swing to Tiger's on the video was both exhilarating and depressing. Compared to Tiger's elegantly efficient movements, my body parts looked like a cocktail party of random chatter.

I'm not suggesting we should eliminate all the small talk from our lives. A certain amount of it probably lubricates social interaction and puts people at ease. However, I imagine that most people, if they were honest with themselves, would admit that they waste far too much time and energy in idle conversations about trivia. If honest, most people would also find that they engaged in a great many trivial conversations because of incompletion. In other words, when we are afraid to talk about what's real and important, we tend to cover up the pain of all that incompletion with small talk and other trivial pursuits.

A PAINFUL BUT ENLIGHTENING MOMENT

Some years ago I had a vivid moment of learning about completion. It occurred while I was walking from the living room to the kitchen in my house. I noticed a pencil on the floor, but I didn't pick it up because I was in a hurry to get to the kitchen to make a cup of coffee. While I was making the cup of coffee, though, I found myself thinking about the pencil. Then I started thinking that I wouldn't be thinking about the pencil if I'd gone ahead and picked it up when I first saw it lying there. I realized that ignoring my initial observation of the pencil had cost me energy. Now, I was expending energy thinking about incompletion when I could have been thinking about something more creative. Here's the punch line of this learning moment: Lost in the labyrinths of my metaphysical inquiry about incompletion, I burned my thumb on the stove!

That moment could serve as a microscopic documentary of the problem with incompletion. To be complete, all I had to do was follow my insight (there's a pencil on the floor) with the essential next action (pick it up). Instead, I skipped the action and carried the incompletion into the kitchen with me. There, the incompletion fueled thoughts about leaving the pencil behind. Further speculation about it led to a (fortunately) minor encounter with physical reality. Why? Because I wasn't present with what was really going on. I was making a cup of coffee in the kitchen while my mind was in the living room picking up a pencil. In the war between physical reality and us, put your money on physical reality every time.

Here's my advice to all of us. If you're walking through your living room and see a dropped pencil, get completion right there on the spot. Pick it up. It doesn't matter who dropped it or why they dropped it or whether they ought to come back and pick it up. If you see it and walk past without picking it up, you leave an incompletion and this drains energy.

How do we determine the next essential action in any given moment? It is always the action that will bring the highest priority project to completion. If a fire had broken out in the kitchen when I dropped the pencil, the highest priority project would have been to put the fire out, not to pick up the pencil. In the context of a fire, a dropped pencil (or even the future possibility of someone stepping on it) is not an essential action.

Think of every interaction of the business day as just this simple. Every conversation, every piece of paper you look at, every tiny little place you focus your attention—each of those moments has an essential next action that will lead to completion. Sometimes the next action is hard to force ourselves to do, but it is always simple and straightforward. For example, if you took something that belonged to somebody else, go ahead and get completion by confessing and giving it back. If you borrowed something and haven't returned it, free up the energy by returning it. Either return it or call the person and ask if you can keep it permanently. It doesn't matter what you do, as long as you get completion.

All it takes is the courage to take the next action, whatever it is. Sometimes, the act of taking the next action can produce living, breathing miracles. Here's one that took a twist no one could have predicted.

A woman who founded and ran a successful business came to me for a day of preretirement coaching a while back. One of her issues was a nagging case of chronic fatigue syndrome. She'd had all the medical workups and many alternative treatments as well, but nothing had chased the symptoms out of her body. I took a different approach. I told her to go someplace where nobody knew her. I suggested she stay there as long as it took to come up with a thorough list of all the incompletions in her life. I knew that incompletions sapped energy from people and organizations quicker than almost anything else. I had also witnessed the power of the First Secret to heal even the most difficult of physical problems.

She borrowed a friend's cabin on Puget Sound and hunkered down for a period of solitude. On the third day she suddenly remembered a huge incompletion from 30 years before. In a fit of spite as she broke up with her first husband, she'd taken a painting worth several thousand dollars. It was an heirloom inheritance from his grandfather and of great sentimental value. Further, she pretended to have nothing to do with its disappearance. Her husband eventually reported it stolen. Ironically, it was indeed stolen from her several years later in a burglary of her storage shed.

Sobbing, she called me from a pay phone at a country store on Puget Sound. What should she do?

I asked if her ex-husband was still alive, and she said she was quite sure he was. I told her to call him and tell him what happened, including the chronic fatigue and my solitude-and-completion prescription. I asked her to call me back to report after she'd finished talking to him.

About 20 minutes later she called back. She'd tracked down her first husband (who was now in his seventies) on a boat in Florida. She had poured out the story, expecting a blast of rage from him in return. Instead, she got a "Thanks" and a chuckle. He told her he'd always known she took it, but that he considered losing it to be a fitting punishment for all the guff he'd given her during the marriage. Plus, he said, he knew her guilt would be punishment enough.

Pretty good story so far, isn't it? Hold on to your hat, though—it gets better. In fact, it has not one but two magical endings.

She asked for his forgiveness, which he promptly gave her. Then, she offered to repay him whatever the painting was worth. She even offered to try to track down the painting. He declined this offer, though, telling her that he knew for a fact that it was unnecessary.

"Why?" she asked.

There was a very simple reason: He had the painting on the wall of his den back at his house! He had seen it in an art auction on the Internet and got it for $800! He'd been the only bidder.

She was now laughing and sobbing as she told me this wonderful outcome. I suggested she send him $1,000, with instructions to cash it or send it on to one of his favorite charities.

I mentioned there were two magical endings. The second, which you may already have guessed, is that her chronic fatigue syndrome disappeared completely. Years later she's still feeling hale and hearty, thanks to the First Secret.

A WORD OF CAUTION ABOUT CRISIS

When a crisis erupts it is natural to leave incomplete your current task to handle the more pressing issue. Then the question becomes: When the crisis has been handled, will we come back to complete the original task? This issue is so important, especially in business, that I want to discuss it carefully with you. First, we all have to develop our own system of prioritizing, so that we'll know what counts as a crisis. My definition revolves around cost assessment. The highest cost is loss of life and limb, so anything that might cause injury or worse automatically trumps whatever else I'm doing. Further down the scale are things that might cost self-esteem. If something occurs that appears to be causing loss of self-esteem, I will stop whatever else I'm doing in order to handle it. For example, I was working on this book one day when I looked out the window and saw my gardener berating an underling in what I considered to be an abusive manner. I saw what the young man had done (he'd run the mower too close to a shrub, whacking off a chunk of the bush), and although it was careless it certainly was not a hanging offense.

I left the cool confines of my office and went out into the blazing sun to intervene. I asked the gardener to ease up, and he responded with a litany of offenses the boy had committed. Although the boy didn't speak much English, he got the gist of what was going on. He shot me a quick grin that communicated volumes. It said, "Thanks, but don't rock the boat because I need this job." I suddenly realized he was an undocumented alien, and that getting berated by his employer was a low-priority issue compared to losing the day's pay.

Everybody eventually cooled down and I went back to work. On the surface it wouldn't seem that handling a gardening issue would be a higher-priority matter than working on my book. However, witnessing the scene stirred up something in me that would have felt incomplete had I not gone out to talk to the gardener. When I came back to my writing the stirred-up feeling was gone, and I was at ease to return to my original task.

My big caution about crisis is based on observations in my own life and hundreds of business consultations: Be careful not to let crisis become an excuse for not completing the things you were working on before the crisis occurred. Crisis has an adrenaline charge to it, and adrenaline is one of the most addictive drugs on earth. It is easy to become addicted to the adrenaline fix of crisis, so that more and more crises are required to feel fully alive. I cannot count the number of times I've heard statements like the following:

"I couldn't finish my degree because I got transferred."

"I couldn't complete the book because we had a baby."

"I couldn't get the report to you because Jack pulled me in to work on the computer crash."

Most of the things I used to call crises really aren't. They're just things that need to be done, and many of them are simply things that *I don't want to do*. My level of resistance to doing them turns them into a crisis. Granted, there have been big, unpleasant events in my life that took time and energy to handle. One that comes to mind from 30 years ago still seems like the biggest crisis of my life. My first marriage, which had been teetering on the brink for a year, broke up suddenly while I was in the last year of completing my Ph.D. I was working two jobs to get by, spending every spare moment working on my doctoral dissertation, when my wife shocked me by announcing that she was leaving for Europe. I found myself within a few days taking on the biggest job of all: single parent to my 4-year-old daughter.

Those next 6 months were the most unhappy and insanely busy time in my life. They were also months of incredible fulfillment, because I got to know my daughter in a way that I would probably never have done had the crisis not happened. I also developed a heartfelt respect and compassion for single parents, to whom I'd never given a moment's thought until I became one.

One moment turned the crisis into a triumph, and it speaks directly to our First Secret. One night I was slumped in a stupor of exhaustion in our tiny grad-student apartment. I'd just bathed my daughter and put her to bed. I went out to sit on the front steps to enjoy my first moments of solitude. As I sat there, I found myself thinking a terribly seductive thought: Why not just abandon my Ph.D. and take the kind of job I had before? I desperately wanted to get my Ph.D. so I could become a clinical and counseling psychologist, but I also wanted some peace in my life. I knew I could get a decent job as a school counselor, and even though it would involve the sacrifice of a dream, it would enable me to work normal hours.

Suddenly a bolt of insight shot through me: I didn't have to complete my whole Ph.D.! *All I had to do was go and finish typing the page I had been working on early that morning before my daughter woke up!* I laughed out loud. It was probably like an alcoholic must feel when he or she realizes, "Hey, I don't have to stay sober my whole life—I just have to stay sober TODAY!"

So, I went in and finished typing that page. The next day I did another one, and one after that. One fine day, 6 months later, I turned in all 225 pages of my dissertation, neatly bound and ready for posterity. As if by magic, my soon-to-be ex-wife returned from Europe shortly after I received my Ph.D. Although I was devastated when she left, I now look upon that 6 months of challenge as one of the greatest gifts of my life.

THE BOTTOM LINE

In golf, stay in relationship with the ball until it's no longer there. Finish your essential business before you peek at the results.

In business and life, finish one key thing before you go on to the next key thing. Complete the task before you concern yourself with the results. Keep a pure and simple focus on the central task, and when you finally look up to check your results, you may find you have created something unimaginably fine. Do this long enough and you may awaken one day to find yourself suffering from chronic delight syndrome.

PRACTICE SESSION

Putting the First Secret into Play

APPLYING THE FIRST SECRET TO BUSINESS AND LIFE

Now I'd like you to take your mind off golf for a few minutes. Give yourself a moment to rest and digest. Let me talk to you about the big implications of this simple wisdom we've been working with.

I'm going to take off my golf cap and put on my psychologist's hat. I've been working with people as a therapist, counselor and executive coach since 1968. In that time I've watched the First Secret help thousands of people lead happier lives and be more successful in business.

Let's focus specifically on business. From coaching executives from about a hundred companies, I can tell you something about business that I had trouble believing when I first realized it: Success and failure in business has almost nothing to do with business per se. That's right—you heard me correctly. Whether you succeed as a businessperson has very little to do with the typical business-related stuff like budgets and marketing. However, it has a great deal to do with completion and follow-through. Ultimately, the First Secret is the major determinant of success in business and life.

Success in business and life depends on doing what you say you'll do. It has to do with keeping agreements—agreements with yourself and agreements with other people. There are lots of other things involved in success, but if you don't keep your agreements you can have all the other stuff and still make an incredible mess out of everything you touch.

Think of making an agreement as being like teeing up a ball. You have to complete that agreement impeccably before you go on to the next thing. If you don't, you leave a loose end undone. Leave a bunch of loose ends around and you end up in the rough of life. Let me give you a personal example from one of our favorite subjects, money.

I've found that forgiving debts is a powerful boost to my bank account as well as my spirits. Logically, one would think that forgiving a debt of $35,000 would make one's bank account $35,000 lighter in the long run. However, this is a linear, Newtonian view that overlooks the powerful effect of the freed-up energy you liberate when you forgive a debt. For example, for three years I "carried" a person who owed me $35,000. He was supposed to pay me back by June 1 of a certain year, and 3 years later I was still getting irregular "payments" in the form of excellent excuses why he couldn't pay me back. I believe that the phrase "carrying a debt" is quite literal—I could feel in my body the strain of the incomplete agreement between me and the other person. It felt like a weight we were both carrying, kind of like a big wet blanket we were forced to share.

Finally, I realized that it could go on this way for a long time. Since I'd been trying to call in the debt for years without success, it seemed that I wasn't likely to get the money anytime soon. So, why not forgive it and move on?

I sat down on the spot and made a new deal with the universe. I got willing to collect at least $35,000 worth of wisdom from the experience. I also opened up to getting my money back, with interest, from some other source. I wrote the person a note, telling him that the debt was now cancelled. I told him briefly that I felt angry and sad about the way it turned out, but that I took full responsibility for my decision to loan him the money. If he wished someday to pay me back, he was welcome to do so, but for reasons of his own and not for any debt he owed me. Further, I told him that I hoped he would also take responsibility for his part in not repaying the debt, but that I absolved him from any blame on my part.

Then, a most remarkable thing happened.

The moment I sent the note, I felt an incredible lightness and new energy flow through me. Within 10 days I reaped a more tangible benefit. A deal unexpectedly dropped into my lap that brought me more than $100,000 with no effort whatsoever. I couldn't help but notice the coincidence. I let go of $35,000 (money I didn't have and wasn't likely to get) and ended the month with 100,000 real dollars more than I started with. I have forgiven a number of debts since then, for amounts ranging from $2,000 to a little over $100,000, and each time my real wealth has grown. I believe that it grew partly as a result of freeing up the energy bound in the debt.

I should mention here that I am far from a starry-eyed true believer in things of a mystical nature. In fact, I am known among both my hard-science and New Age friends as the skeptic's skeptic. I'm the guy they always call to ask things like "What about this electro-acupuncture stuff? Is there any scientific evidence for it?" However, I always keep the most open mind I can muster in every situation. It's a mysterious world we live in, as well as a plain-as-day one.

Forgiving debts is not an exact science, so you may not get exactly the same results I got. I believe it has a great deal to do with the intention with which you forgive them. If there's any rancor remaining in you when you forgive the debt, you'll probably get an equal measure of rancor in the outcome.

Think of completion like an electrical circuit. If you don't close the circuit, you leave a loose charge looking around for a place to land. Every time we fail to make a completion, we leave another circuit open. Pretty soon all our juice is being wasted, frittered away in unproductive sputters, short-circuiting all our other projects.

Being impeccable in completing things, especially making and keeping agreements, is the absolute fundamental success key to business and life.

Success in business depends also on whether you can inspire other people to make agreements and complete them. One of the biggest mistakes I see in the business world is failure to get meaningful agreements in place.

Listen to a manager before and after I coached him on how to get agreements in place. These excerpts are from tapes of meetings—I've bleeped out some details to maintain privacy.

BEFORE LEARNING THE SECRET

MANAGER: Okay, so let's get back together on Friday afternoon and go over the fall schedule again. I'd like all of you to bring in your figures to work with.

(He stood up abruptly, nodded to everybody and darted out.)

This meeting resulted in a flurry of phone calls back and forth because he didn't pin down exactly what time on Friday the meeting was to be held. He also didn't get buy-in from everybody that they would have their figures by the appointed time. In short, he didn't reach completion. It cost everybody. First, there was the wasted energy and minutes of all the phone calls. Then, one person was late for the Friday meeting because he didn't pick up his messages, and two others didn't have the necessary numbers.

Everybody had plenty of excuses, though, and the Friday meeting turned into a growling match.

AFTER LEARNING THE SECRET

MANAGER: *I'd like to schedule our next meeting for tomorrow at 1 P.M. Would everyone look at their calendar and make sure they can get here so that we can start promptly?*

(Everybody looked.)

MANAGER: *Bob, I notice a scowl—do you have a conflict?*

BOB: *Oh! Thanks for noticing. Yeah, well, my wife's having knee surgery at 4 and I'd like to get out of here in plenty of time so that I can take her.*

MANAGER: *Can everybody meet at 12:30 then? That should give us plenty of time to finish before Bob needs to leave.*

(Everybody nodded—Bob smiled and thanked them.)

MANAGER: *Would everybody agree to bring expense reports, too?*

(Everybody nodded.)

MANAGER: *Okay, so we're on for tomorrow at 12:30, expense reports in hand. Any questions or things we need to consider before then?*

(Everybody shook his or her head.)

MANAGER: *Okay, thanks.*

A tremendous amount of energy is wasted in business because of loose agreements. I can't count the number of times I've heard things like:

"Did we say 4 or 4:30?"

"Let's see, were we supposed to have our expense vouchers in by Friday or Monday?"

"Where is everybody? Weren't we meeting at noon?"

Taken individually, moments like these are trivial. However, in the course of a day or a week or a life, they constitute a major energy drain that saps our creative juices.

To live in a state of completion is a great and noble goal of human living—it is unlikely that any of us will achieve anything close to perfection in that realm, but it needs to become the target we aim for every day.

Practically speaking, it's not that hard. There are only a few things to keep our focus on:

- Completion is when we acknowledge the feelings we have inside. If we're scared, we look at the fear steadily until we find out if there's anything we need to do about it. If we're sad, we pause to honor whatever loss we're grieving. If we're angry, we look for the trespass that triggered it or the internal rigidity of our own that's recycling it.

   You don't have to act on all your feelings, but it's essential to let yourself know when you're feeling them. Knowing yourself—your feelings, needs and motivations—allows you to walk through the world in a state of inner completion.

- In our conversations with others, completion is when we say the essential thing that needs to be said. In a given conversation there may be a dozen different subjects discussed, but if there's an essential one that's not discussed, there's an incompletion hovering in the air.

If I say, "Honey, it's sure hot today" and "Honey, let's have fried chicken for dinner" but forget to say, "Honey, I'm having an affair," I can be pretty sure I've left something essential incomplete. In truth, the whole interchange took place in a context of incompletion, because my life would have become one big incompletion the moment the affair started.

• Completion is making good on agreements you've made. A great deal of wasted energy in business is stirred up around sloppy agreements and broken agreements. When we fail to make clean agreements, we forfeit the right to expect anything to go well, even a trip to the convenience store. When we fail to make good on agreements, we not only forfeit the right to expect things to go well, we virtually guarantee chaos and upset. In the chaotic energy of upset, blame is spewed and excuses are made. Success in business depends on whether you can step out of the blame-and-excuses game and into complete, impeccable accountability.

I'd like to hear a politician say, just once,

something like this: "I take full responsibility for the way the budget talks are going. I know it may look like the other party is working against me, but it's my job to get the job done and I'm not doing it. I'm looking at how I'm creating obstacles by the way I'm going about it, and I'm working overtime to figure out how we can get it to work."

Remember that I said there were huge implications to all of this? Well, I believe that what we're talking about has the biggest of all implications: It's about where we stand with ourselves, with our fellow humans, with the earth and its inhabitants, with the cosmos and its Creator.

There is a word in the Navajo language, *hakomi*, that can be translated as something like "how we stand in relation to all the worlds." In fact, a friend of mine, Ron Kurtz, calls the form of psychotherapy he developed by this name. You can say *hakomi* as a greeting, asking the other person "How do you stand in relation to all your worlds?" You're asking the person to do a deep check-in: Are you in harmony with your inner world, your feelings, your dreams?

Are you in harmony with your loved ones, your community? Are you in harmony with your Creator?

As we walk through life, we are walking through many worlds. The First Secret counsels us to aim for completion with all our worlds.

In conversations with Navajo and other Native American spiritual teachers, I've learned a great deal about the value of completion as a spiritual practice. One of the highest ideals in Native American spiritual teachings is an inner feeling of connection with ourselves, other people and the living world around us. My own experience has shown me the reality of this wisdom. Every deep spiritual experience of my life has deepened a feeling of connection in me. On one exalted occasion, during a meditative walk in the high desert, I felt so connected to the earth around me that it seemed as though the universe and I were breathing in unison. On another occasion, during a seminar on conscious golf and business, a man came over to me with golf club in hand and a glow in his eyes.

He gestured to his club and said, "We're both the same thing." I urged him to say more.

"A moment ago, during the 'swinging' exercise (the same one you'll find in the next chapter), I suddenly realized that the club and I are exactly the same. It's metal and I'm a person, but we're both just different expressions of the same thing—everything is all one thing."

Here was an insurance executive who, in a moment of deep connection, had turned into a mystic. All I could say was "Yes!"

All it takes is one such moment to deepen our appreciation of every successive moment of our lives. Although I have thrived on many such experiences, I yearn for more. To be honest, I would like to enjoy that deep sense of connection in every moment of my life. I'm not there yet, but then I still have a few rounds to play.

Incompletion is a major barrier to the feeling of connection. Specific questions can help us address various levels of incompletion.

• Is there anything in our inner world we are avoiding facing?

• Are there unexplored feelings or unfulfilled goals that gnaw at us?

If so, we will remain unsettled in a state of incompletion until we embrace those feelings and take steps toward fulfilling those goals.

• Are we complete with our circle of friends and family? Have we spoken what's in our hearts to our friends and family (and listened carefully to what's in theirs)?

• Do we feel in harmony with spirit, God, the Creator force, or whatever we may call it?

Ultimately our sense of spirituality is determined by how completely we have embraced the wholeness of ourselves and the world around us. The Native American ideal is to honor to spirit of the earth and the Great Spirit that enlivens the cosmos.

With every golf swing and with every moment of life, we face the same choice. We can immerse ourselves in the process until we have completed it impeccably, or we can jump ahead prematurely to peek at the outcome.

The bottom-line truth is this: Human beings feel good when we complete things. When we don't, we don't.

Given this simple truth, why isn't completing things more popular?

Why do we walk away from conversations leaving significant things unspoken?

Why do we forget to do things we said we'd do?

Why do we promise and not deliver, or deliver and not get paid?

The reason: Human beings fear completing things. Based on my 30 years of working with people, I think it's partly because of our innate dread of death. Completing things means we're finished, and being finished means we're going to die. Most of us haven't made friends with that notion. Our unconscious mind thinks that we can cheat death through incompletion—if we leave enough things undone, we make ourselves immortal. Unfortunately for us, it just means we make ourselves miserable.

The same issue causes us to fear other things, such as pain, conflict and loss. We often avoid facing those things fully, and the choice to turn away from them costs us dearly. Instead of handling a conflict in 10 minutes, for example, we stretch it out over 10 years. Or take the example of actual, physical pain. Some years ago I learned a life lesson about pain in working with an enlightened dentist. When I say enlightened, I mean that he was wide-open to new human possibilities as well as being a trained Buddhist meditator. I mentioned to him in our first session that the only thing I didn't like about going to the dentist was the numbness from the novocaine. He said that some patients, including himself, just used deep breathing and meditation instead of anesthetic for their pain. He said that a lot of pain is simply caused by the intense resistance that the patient mounts by tensing against the sensations.

I took the challenge (though not without considerable trepidation). As the drill whined and bit in, I breathed deeper and let my belly muscles relax. Each time I felt pain, I continued to soften my belly and slow my breathing. Remarkably, as I did this I felt the pain turn into "just sensation." The more I breathed and relaxed, the more the pain would recede into a not-unpleasant blur of different sensations.

I left his office feeling great. Not only did I learn a powerful new technique for handling pain in my life, I learned a major lesson about life itself: It's often not the thing itself that hurts; it's my resistance to it that makes it hurt. (My friend Buddy Winston, writer for Jay Leno, heard my story and suggested that I was "Transcending Dental Medication.")

We fear the absoluteness of completion because we fear the absoluteness of death. So, we keep ourselves stirred up by leaving a mess of incompletions lying about. This stirred-up feeling, whether we call it excitement or anxiety, also keeps us from staying focused long enough to look at death and say, "All right."

We need to grow up and get comfortable with dying. We need to grow up and learn the real truth: Completing things makes us feel serene and whole. Based on up-close work with more than twenty thousand people, I have concluded that we humans fear serenity and wholeness more than we fear chaos and incompletion. Be honest—how many days have you spent in your life feeling completely serene and whole? How many hours even? Some people have told me they haven't felt a minute of natural serenity in their adult lives.

I want more from life than that, and I want more than that for you, too. Let's find out together if we can overcome our fear of completion so we can welcome more serenity into our lives.

Let's aim for genuine serenity in every moment. To do that, we must turn every moment into a quest for completion.

That's the First Secret of hitting a superb golf shot, doing good business and living a splendid life.

INTRODUCING THE KEY PRACTICES

Three practices help you put the three secrets to work. None of the practices takes longer than a few minutes to carry out, and each produces powerful results that you can readily see from the first time you do it.

The first practice gives you the focus you need to stay on track all day. The second practice gets you into the essential flow. Without focus, flow has little usefulness in the real world. When you're in the flow, you enjoy an easy feeling of energy and harmony inside you. When you're focused correctly, your flow has purpose and direction to it. There are times, however, when both your focus and your flow disappear. That's when the third practice saves the day. The third practice shows you how to deal with the inevitable surprises and changes of any business day or round of golf. When you know how to ride the rapids of change, you can preserve your flow and focus through the vicissitudes of a typical busy day.

Any powerful practice carries risks, and these practices are no exception. If you do these practices every day, you run the risk of enhancing your magnificence to dangerous levels. People around you may become so dazzled by your magnificence that they may tend to break out in a profuse sweat or operate machinery in an unsafe manner. If this sort of thing begins to happen, shave a few minutes off your daily practice.

I've been at the executive-coaching business a lot longer than I've been playing golf. I did my first session with a corporate executive in the early 1970s, but I didn't play a round of golf until 20 years later. I worked out the following practices in the rough-and-tumble world of daily business life, for the practical purpose of helping executives relieve stress, stay focused and operate at a higher level of effectiveness. Years later, I was surprised and pleased to discover that the very same practices, if modified slightly, could make a big contribution to golfers.

These practices mean a great deal to me personally. They've added immeasurable value to my own life, as well as to the lives of the people to whom my colleagues and I have taught them. They are exactly the same practices you would learn if you came to the introductory course at our Academy of Conscious Business and Golf.

Because I'm giving them to you here at a steep discount (compared to the $1,000 you'd be spending if you came to the live seminar), I'd like you to match me with $1,000 of your commitment. I invite you to give these practices a fair trial by using them for a week. You may have heard of Ivy Lee, who coached many top executives in the first half of the twentieth century. The head of U.S. Steel invited Mr. Lee to follow him around for a few days in order to make recommendations on how the executive might improve his effectiveness. After doing so, Mr. Lee said he had one major recommendation to make. He said that if the executive would spend 5 minutes doing one particular thing at the beginning of the day, his effectiveness would grow by leaps and bounds. The executive asked what it was, and Mr. Lee offered him the following deal. Mr. Lee said he'd give it to him, but only if the executive would promise to do it every day for 2 weeks. At the end of the 2 weeks of fair trial, the executive could stop doing it if he didn't find it useful. Mr. Lee went even further—if the executive didn't find it useful, he didn't have to pay him a nickel for any of his consulting services. However, if the executive did find it useful, he could write him a check for any amount the executive thought it was worth.

The executive took the deal.

Mr. Lee told the executive to spend 5 minutes each morning generating a simple "to do" list, then update it throughout the day. The executive practiced it faithfully as promised for 2 weeks. When Mr. Lee went in to check the results, the executive handed him $25,000. This event took place in the early part of the century, when you could get a brand-new car for $1,500. The fee Mr. Lee collected would be the equivalent in today's money of nearly $250,000.

I offer you the following practices in the spirit of Mr. Lee, and I will tender our nonprofit wing, The Foundation for Conscious Living, as a possibly recipient of any tangible expression of your gratitude for them.

YOUR 5-MINUTE DAILY PRACTICE
FOR MASTERING THE FIRST SECRET

The Business Practice: The Completions Card

The highest-leverage few minutes of your business day is the time you spend working on your Completions Card. I urge you to give it a 1-week fair trial, using it scrupulously every day. Everyone I've known who's done so has become a passionate advocate for its benefits. The reason: It frees up a tremendous amount of energy, which can then be channeled into whatever creative activities you choose.

You can download the official version of the Completions Card free from www.consciousgolf.biz. If you want to make your own, all you need is a 3- by 5-inch card. Actually, you're welcome to make it any size you like, but we use the 3- by 5-inch size because it fits easily into a pocket and has emerged as the most-used format.

The Completions Card is a multidimensional "to do" list. It helps you go deep as well as fast. If you're serious about moving at maximum speed while living a high-quality life, you can make a great leap forward by beginning each day with a few minutes of work on your Completions Card.

Here's what it looks like:

COMPLETIONS

Today's Top 5 Essential Actions

1.

2.

3.

4.

5.

Are there any situations/people I've been avoiding facing directly? List and add actions to the Top 5 if warranted.

_____

Are there any choices I've been avoiding making? List and add actions to the Top 5 if warranted.

_____

Do I need to make any new agreements?
(Or acknowledge any previous agreements broken or unfulfilled?) List and add. . . .

_____

_____

_____

Do I need to speak any significant truths to people I can reach today? (Or speak any withheld truths from before today?) List and add. . . .

_____

_____

_____

Do I have feelings I need to acknowledge in myself or others?

| anger | sadness | fear |
| excitement | joy | sexual |

Are there appreciations I can speak
to people today? List and add. . . .

___

The Elements of the Completions Card

Let's go through each element carefully, so that you'll
know exactly how to work your Completions Card.

Top 5 Actions

My colleagues and I have found that nearly everyone
has at least five key actions that they need to carry out
during the day. If they complete those actions, they
feel good. If they don't, they don't.

Your unconscious mind and your body already
know what those actions are. You may have even
dreamed about them during the night. The Completions Card gives you a place to bring them to conscious
awareness, which frees up the energy to get more done.

Some of your Top 5 actions may be quick and
simple:

• Get Joanne's birthday present.

• Complete memo to Bob about the reorganiza-
tion of the Charleston office.

Others may be more complex and require carrying over to subsequent days:

- Schedule meetings of the Planning Committee through end of year.

- Assemble compensation package for Leo.

However, even the most complex task always has an essential next action. The moment you think about and write down your Top 5 essential actions for the day, you free up energy for carrying out those tasks. Your unconscious mind won't have to keep sorting and filing and reminding you all day long.

Practically speaking, we've found that the ideal number of actions to write down at one time is five. If you finish those five by 8 A.M., write another Top 5. I often go through several Completions Cards during the course of the day.

Facing

An enormous amount of your energy gets consumed by avoiding crucial situations that need to be faced directly and dealt with. I once put off having an essential conversation with an employee for days. I dreaded her reaction, my having to deal with her reaction and all the various ramifications of it. I put it off for several days, but on the morning of the fourth day I woke up groaning and thinking about it. I didn't realize I was groaning until my wife asked me, "What were you groaning about just before you woke up this morning?" Part of me was already dreading the conversation and groaning about it, even though my conscious "I" hadn't come awake yet.

That's why we need to face things as soon as possible. Each time we avoid facing something essential, our bodies have to carry the burden of the avoidance. Avoid things long enough and our whole existence becomes one long, drawn-out groan.

When I do corporate consultations and executive coaching, I use my "$10,000 questions." I call them by that name because I (and the colleagues who work with me) get paid that amount for a day of asking them. Most of my $10,000 questions are on the Completions Card, and the "Facing question" may be the most valuable of all.

I've asked this question of thousands of people, including many whose names and faces you'd instantly recognize. I can tell you that almost nobody likes this question when I ask it, but I can also tell you that almost everybody tells me later that it was a turning point. The moment you turn to face something you've been avoiding is the moment you get your life back.

I want you to go far beyond that, however. I want you to make a habit of asking these $10,000 questions. In fact, I want you to live inside these questions and let them live inside you. In other words, make them a lifestyle instead of just a lifeline.

What have you been avoiding facing? What is the thing you've been avoiding that would give you a quantum leap in energy and creativity if you faced it directly?

Don't worry if you don't get an immediate answer. When I ask an executive this question, I do not expect a verbal answer right away. I watch carefully, though, for the whole-body answer. I watch especially carefully for any defensive reaction to this question. For example, does the person flinch when I ask it? Does he frown and get critical? Does she fire back at me a hostile question, such as "What does that have to do with anything!?"

Sometimes, defensive reactions are much more subtle. For example, the person may ask me to explain further or may critique the way I asked the question.

The bottom line, though, is that any reaction other than reflecting on the question should be considered a defensive reaction. It takes the same amount of time to ask for an explanation or have a hostile reaction as it does to reflect, wonder and possibly get an answer. By engaging in the defensive reaction, no matter how noisy or quiet, you waste time during which you could have been wondering and learning.

To help put defensive reactions into perspective, please look carefully at the scale on pages 94 and 95. I developed it many years ago to help people understand their defenses. By seeing their typical defenses on paper, they are able to move through them quickly toward openness to learning.

This scale is designed specifically for use in situations where people are giving feedback to each other. However, it can be applied to any situation where people might tend to get defensive. Believe me, people tend to get defensive when I ask them questions such as "What do you most need to face directly that you've been avoiding facing?" That's a good thing, though, because it's good for all of us to discover where, when and why we get defensive. If we get defensive when someone asks us what we need to be facing, it simply means we have been avoiding facing something important. If that were not the case, we would have no reason to get defensive.

Think of Bill Clinton clenching his jaw, wagging his finger and saying, "I didn't have sex with that woman!" This was a classic defensive reaction: Look on the scale at −2, −3 and −7. If he hadn't been guilty as charged, he would not have needed to defend himself by self-righteous indignation or any other means. Imagine instead if he had gone to a +1 or all the way to a +9 or +10 in response to the same question.

QUESTIONER AT NEWS CONFERENCE: *There are rumors going around that you and Monica had a sexual relationship. Is that true?*

CLINTON: *Thanks for asking. [+4] I've been talking about this with my wife and a therapist, but it looks like it's time to talk about it publicly. Yes, the rumor is true, and I have been working on how and why I created this kind of event in my life. [+8]*

QUESTIONER: *What are you going to do about it?*

(continued on page 96)

HIGH OPENNESS TO LEARNING

+10 Implementing (planning actions, requesting support for follow-up).

+9 Feeling and showing genuine enthusiasm about the possibilities.

+8 Taking full responsibility for the issue, the results that were created.

+7 Thinking out loud, making new associations about the issue.

+6 Requesting information and examples about the issue.

+5 Listening generously (paraphrasing the other person's statements without interjecting your point of view).

+4 Expressing appreciation for the messenger and the message, regardless of delivery.

+3 Openly wondering about the issue.

+2 Expressing genuine curiosity about the issue.

+1 Demonstrating open posture.

THE KEY TRANSITION MOVE:
Choosing Wondering over Defending;
Committing to Learning

-1 Showing polite interest outwardly while inwardly clinging to your point of view and/or rehearsal rebuttal; feeling bored.

-2 Explaining how the person has misperceived the situation.

-3 Interpreting what the person is saying as an attack.

-4 Justifying why you're the way you are or acted the way you did.

-5 Going silent, cryptic with answers, or getting edgy, snappy or frustrated (feeling "put-upon").

-6 Finding fault with the way the message is being delivered.

-7 Righteous indignation; demanding evidence in a hostile manner.

-8 Blaming someone or something else.

-9 Attacking or threatening the messenger, verbally or otherwise.

-10 Creating uproar or making an abrupt departure.

LOW OPENNESS TO LEARNING

CLINTON: *First I'm going to focus on healing it in myself. I'd also like to ask for your help—all of you in the media, in Congress and in the country—to do it with me. Turn the searchlight of awareness onto yourself and ask yourself if you have any breaches of integrity in the sexual realm or anywhere else in your life. Let's turn this into an opportunity to create a culture of integrity. Today I'll be asking Congress to create a Cabinet-level Secretary for Integrity. [+10]*

I would be proud to vote for a politician who talked like that.

Choosing and Deciding

Facing is usually the first step in solving any problem or handling any situation. Choosing or making a decision is often the crucial next step. Many of us rob ourselves of our energy every day by avoiding choices and decisions we need to make. Avoiding choices can have life-threatening consequences for ourselves and others—Shakespeare's *Hamlet*, one of the most staged plays in history, documents brilliantly the unpleasant consequences of delaying essential choices. By the end of the play there are bodies all over the stage, in-cluding the hero's.

Most of our choices probably won't cost quite as much as Hamlet's if we avoid them, but cost us they will. We sap our energy by delaying decisions, and the longer we delay them, the more we drain ourselves. Making the delayed choice gives you your energy back.

Agreements

The failure to make and keep clear agreements causes a great deal of human misery. Breaking agreements probably creates the most stress, and the stress gets worse when we avoid facing the people who have been inconvenienced by our broken agreements. There is a universal tendency to sweep broken agreements under the rug and hope nobody notices. However, as Tom Peters says, "There is no such thing as a minor lapse of integrity." Like it or not, says one of my fa-vorite sages, Rabbi Nachmann, "All words are counted and charged."

Human beings are a great deal more sensitive than many of us probably think. We register when people break agreements with us, although we often register it unconsciously. We also register when we break agreements with others. Then, to drown out the "noise" in our bodies—the noise that is actually the body's attempt to tell us something is wrong—we try to pretend everything is just fine.

One of the most important things any of us can do each day is to focus on our agreements. Your Completions Card will help keep this crucial point in your awareness.

Truth

Here's my conclusion, drawn from working with people for 30 years: Absolute honesty is not only the best policy but also the best way to enhance the flow of good feeling inside ourselves and with others. Honesty will also help you get a good night's sleep. If you're not feeling in the flow, or if you're having trouble sleeping, look for a significant truth you need to communicate with someone.

If there is any significant truth we haven't communicated to a key person, we forfeit the right to expect a good relationship with that person. Most people don't know this simple principle. When things aren't going well in the relationship, they look to the other person as the source of what's wrong.

Often, the truths are very simple:

- "I'm angry about _____."

- "I'm hurt about _____."

- "I'm scared that _____."

- "I really want _____ and I'm afraid to tell you."

I've found that the most significant truths—the ones that really get the flow of energy restored—almost never take longer than 10 seconds to speak. However, I've seen people avoid those 10 seconds for decades.

When I ask them, most people tell me they haven't been honest with the other person because the person "really doesn't want to hear the truth" or because "I don't want to hurt her/him." Sometimes they tell me the other person "isn't safe" to tell the truth to. When they get under these superficial reasons, the reason usually turns out to be "I haven't told the truth because I don't want to face the consequences." Under that is a primal fear that all of us need to acknowledge: "I haven't told the truth because I fear living at the highest level of creativity and energy, and lying is one way I've learned that will reliably dampen my energy."

Honesty, then, is the path to living at the peak flow of creativity and productivity. It restores harmony to our system—literally hundreds of people have told me that they got their first good night's sleep after finally telling a significant truth they'd been avoiding.

People dread telling the truth because they fear the consequences, but in actual fact, I've only seen positive consequences in the long run for being honest. There is usually a short-term flurry of upset about it, but the ultimate outcome is usually a more stable and higher-functioning relationship.

The Acid Test

The best question to assess the health of any relationship is this: Is there anything significant I've discussed with a third party (friend, minister, therapist) that I haven't talked to the primary person about? For example, if I've stolen money from Jim, have I discussed this with my wife or my lawyer but not with Jim? If I've cheated on my wife, have I told others about it but not my wife?

In one memorable session of couples' counseling

some years ago, my wife (psychologist Dr. Kathlyn Hendricks) learned that the husband had discussed his infidelities with several male friends, several female friends, his attorney and his squash partner. However, he said he had never even considered telling his wife. The reason he gave: He didn't want to destroy the trust between them! Kathlyn, in her gentle way, pointed out that the trust between them had actually been destroyed with the first infidelity. Not telling his wife only compounded the trust problem.

This is a classic example of the problem that many of us carry around: We want to act as if our massive integrity breaches are having no effect on business as usual. This idea is based on a false equation: that hiding a lie carefully is the same as not lying.

Fortunately for all of us, our bodies don't lie. Our bodies will send clear signals in the form of anxiety, depression and physical pain when we hide our lies for too long.

Tips on Communicating Withheld Truths
From facilitating hundreds of truth-telling sessions in business and domestic situations, I have several practical suggestions for you.

• Don't do it while you or the other person is driving, operating equipment or doing anything where an upset could cause physical injury.

• Don't use liquor or other drugs to loosen yourself up beforehand. This sends the wrong message to your body: that you can't be honest unless you're chemically altered. Our bodies need to know that they can be honest all the time.

• Don't think it has anything to do with the other person. If you've been thinking the other person "isn't safe" or "doesn't want to hear it," you're missing the point. It's really about us and our fear of living at the highest level of integrity and positive energy.

Feelings

Unacknowledged feelings are a major source of stress. In fact, my colleague David Hubbard, M.D., who has treated more than five thousand cases of migraine, back pain and other chronic pain, believes that the act of hiding significant feelings like anger and sadness is the major cause of chronic pain. Your body may experience anger, for example, about something that occurs in a conversation at breakfast. You push it out of your awareness and go about business as usual. At noon, your body communicates with you in a more forceful way, by sending you a twinge of back pain or a dull headache.

Compare the act of hiding emotions to another feeling we're all familiar with: bladder tension. If I ignore the first signals of bladder tension, I can be sure that the twinges will come back later in a stronger form. The twinges are trying to communicate something important to me of an action that must be taken. If I continue to ignore it, it certainly doesn't go away.

However, many of the people I work with think that their emotions will go away if they ignore them. We would never think of applying this misguided philosophy to bladder tension. The reason is that from an early age we've been coached to be sensitive to bladder signals and to act on them. It's socially acceptable to excuse yourself for a moment to act on the signals from bladder tension. It's important to apply this same principle to other feelings, such as anger, sadness and fear. All we usually need to do is be aware of the feeling and talk about it honestly. We need to make it socially acceptable to say, "Excuse me, I'm feeling scared" or "I'm feeling some anger and sadness in my body as we're talking about this subject. Let me tune in to it for a moment so that I can tell you more about it."

Dr. Hubbard is convinced that the ability to have those kinds of short feeling-conversations would save billions of dollars in health-care costs annually.

Appreciations

When is the last time someone has expressed clearly to you something they appreciate about you? When is the last time you've spoken a clear appreciation to another person? I've asked these questions in many different settings: business, family life, friendship. There is abundant scientific evidence that the act of speaking clear, simple appreciations to one another makes us healthier and happier. However, even in light of this evidence, human beings continue to be stingy in expressing appreciation.

Some years ago, during the time I was a professor at the University of Colorado, I came across a study by John Gottman on the power of appreciation in close relationships. John, a respected researcher at the University of Washington, had found that healthy marriages had a 5-to-1 ratio of positive, appreciative messages to negative ones. Troubled marriages had closer to a 1-to-1 ratio. On the way out of a meeting later in the day, I decided to put his findings to use.

I said to a colleague, "I appreciate the way you responded to the dean about the parking issue." She looked at me with furrowed brow and replied, "Why am I suddenly suspicious?"

That's our problem in a nutshell, isn't it? We have grown up in an atmosphere of such stinginess of appreciation that we automatically think something nefarious is afoot if we hear one. I told my colleague about the study I'd read and assured her that I was merely making a small effort to make our faculty relationships more positive. This led to a rich discussion with her, in which she revealed that, in her family, an expression of appreciation was usually followed by some sort of put-down. When I reflected on it, I recalled many such instances myself.

Let's put a stop to all that. Let's make the world safe for appreciation. Begin by thinking of the people you'll see today and what you appreciate about them. Take the risk of telling them simply and clearly what you appreciate.

Your Completions Card will keep you focused on this important area of awareness.

The Key Daily Practice for Golf

Let's apply everything we've been discussing to your golf game. As the First Secret tells us, the focal point of your awareness should be on completing the process of hitting the golf ball. We need to be right with the ball until it isn't there anymore. The first task is to bring the club face into contact with the ball. If we pull our attention away just before we hit the ball, we do not fulfill the purpose of the swing. No completion.

However, hitting the ball is not enough. We need to complete the process of hitting the ball by staying focused on it until it is no longer there. This gives us follow-through. If we peek too soon to see how we did, we pull our attention away at a crucial moment and lose our follow-through. Again, no completion.

Picture a hotel ballroom with a couple hundred people in it. There is an atmosphere of rapt attention—it is utterly silent except for the click and ping of putters striking golf balls. I'm teaching a conscious golf and conscious business workshop at a conference of businesspeople. There's been a cold snap—otherwise we'd be doing our putting outside on the lawn.

I've instructed them to focus on one thing and one thing only: completion. They're doing the same exercise I'd like you to do—it's the golf equivalent of the Completions Card. On the Completions Card, you'll notice that it begins with action and ends with appreciation. That's exactly what I'd like you to do now.

Get a putter and a ball and a small scrap of paper about an inch square. Write YES! on the piece of paper.

Place the ball on the piece of paper. The paper should not be visible beneath the ball.

Address the ball as if you are going to putt it. Before you do, however, remember that there's a piece of paper beneath the ball. You can't see it, of course, but you know it's there. In this exercise there are only two tasks:

1. Hitting the ball

2. Keeping your focus on the ball until it's no longer there and the YES! is revealed

In the hotel ballroom I ask the participants to make ten putts, using the target of a paper cup. I'd like you to select a similar item you can use for a target. A cup or a water glass will do just fine.

Now, here's a crucial instruction. Although you'll be putting to a target, I don't want you to grade yourself on whether you hit the target. I want you to grade yourself on only one variable: whether you kept your focus on the ball until the YES! appeared.

Make ten putts in a row, noting each time how well you did with keeping your focus on the ball until it was no longer there and the YES! appeared. After each putt, take a few seconds to appreciate yourself, regardless of how you did.

Let me tell you what happens in every one of those hotel ballrooms or putting greens where I teach this exercise. Invariably, people start chuckling and experiencing "aha" as the exercise goes along. The reason: They realize that they sink more putts by not trying to get the ball in the hole! In other words, when you focus on completing your stroke (seeing the YES!, not peeking to see how you did), you end up sinking more putts than when you focus on getting the ball in the hole.

That's the First Secret at work.

Remember, on and off the course: Focus on completion, and the job takes care of itself.

CHAPTER 3

THE SECOND SECRET

Now I'd like to show you the Second Secret of hitting a superb golf shot. The Second Secret also gives you an essential skill for enjoying an easeful, successful business day and a life full of natural good feeling.

When you were a kid, did you ever swing on a playground swing set? You probably did, but if you haven't done it yourself, you've probably seen pictures of kids on swing sets. To grasp the Second Secret of the superb golf shot, I'd like you to create an inner playground in your mind. Your imaginary playground comes equipped with swings for you to play on.

I'd like you to imagine sitting down on the seat of a playground swing. You push off with your legs and begin to swing gently forward and back. You go backward on your backswing, then you swoop close to the ground and up into your front-swing. Imagine getting an easy, satisfying swing going back and forth—big and easy and complete. Back and forth you swing—free and fun.

When you feel like taking a break from your imaginary swinging, pause and rest for a moment while I philosophize a little. Let's think about what makes swinging such a favorite of kids all over the world.

First of all, swinging is easy. All you have to do is get yourself started; then gravity does the rest of the work for you.

Second, it feels good. You feel free—you're unfettered by the bounds of gravity. Some of us kids, including your author, have gotten so intoxicated by the freedom and the rushing through space that we forgot to hang on to the chain. We attempted to break free of the bounds of gravity so that we could soar heavenward, there to taste the ultimate exhilaration of truly unfettered flight.

I remember it well.

In my defense, I was only five at the time, and I required only one learning experience for me to hold on for dear life ever after. The scolding by my mother was nothing compared to the short and impactful lesson I got directly from gravity.

So, if you hold on just right, swinging is easy and feels good. Ask a few kids and they'll all tell you—if it isn't easy and it doesn't feel good it's not swinging.

But that's not all. In order to be real swinging, it has to have a third characteristic. It has to be fun.

Fun . . . yes, fun. It has to be fun or it's not swinging. Kids are smart about swinging. If somebody's pushing them too high for it to be fun, they start screaming and want to get off. If it's too fast to be fun, they let us know right away. They know that it has to be fun to be a swing.

Some kids like to be pushed high and fast. They're having fun while they're going high and fast—it's called exhilaration. Big fun. That great, huge, demented grin kids get on a roller coaster is the exhilaration of having fun while you're feeling some fear and some excitement. The psychiatrist Fritz Perls said that fear is only excitement without the breath. I've called his wisdom to mind many times when I've been scared, and it's worked every time.

Let's get back to our inner playground.

I'd like you to get on your imaginary swing and

have some more fun. Remember that swinging is easy and fun and that it feels good. Sit down on your inner swing-seat and imagine swinging back and forth. Keep it easy and fun and full of good feeling.

Now, imagine letting your toes lightly brush the ground as you come through the bottom of your swing. Each time you swing past the ground, brush the ground lightly with your feet. Notice that the moment of touching the ground doesn't interrupt the swing. It's just a small whisk in the fullness of the swing. One whole swing is easy and fun and feels good, with a tiny whisk at the bottom as you touch the ground.

Now, step off your imaginary playground back into real life.

Now, in real life, pick up a golf club if you have one handy. Get your grip established. If you're reading this somewhere away from your golf clubs, you can swing something else or even just your arms. I'll give you the instructions as if you're holding a club.

Sam Snead said that we should hold a golf club like we would hold a live bird. To me, that is a genuinely useful image. I've held living birds in my hands, and perhaps you have, too.

If we were holding a live bird, we would want our hands to transmit a specific message to the bird. The message our grip would say would go something like this: I'm not going to squeeze you so tightly that you'll feel uncomfortable, but you're not going to fly away, either. Play around with your grip until you find that "live bird" feel.

Look around to make sure there's nothing you could damage by swinging the club. Get plenty of space around you so that you can swing the club around in various directions without running into anything. Now close your eyes.

Stand as you would to address a ball, only keep your eyes closed.

Swing the club easily back and forth, just a foot or two, like the pendulum of a clock. Use your "live bird" grip—tell the club with your hands that you're not going to squeeze it uncomfortably but you're not going to let it go, either. Find a grip that is easy and fun and that feels good. Easy swinging. Swinging that feels good. Swinging to have fun.

Make your swing a little bigger now, still keeping your eyes closed. Let the swing be easy and fun and full of good feeling. Remember that feeling of swinging on a playground swing set. Make sure your body recognizes what you're doing as a swing instead of a whack or a chop.

Now, imagine that you were brushing the top of grass with your club. Imagine just brushing the top of the grass so you'd bend it a tiny bit with each swing.

Make the swing a little bigger now. Imagine standing in the tee box. Imagine you are about to hit a golf ball toward the flag in the distance. The flag is the target. Each time you swing your club, imagine flinging the club toward the target. Feel the type of fling that would allow you to toss the club the farthest with the least effort.

The natural, organic golf swing is the same feel as flinging the club toward the target. Keep swinging with your eyes closed, each time getting the feel of flinging the club toward the target.

Gradually wind down now until you are making your original pendulum swing, just a foot or two back and forth.

Finally, come to rest and open your eyes.

You've just learned the Second Secret of hitting a superb golf shot. You've just felt the Second Secret of leading a successful life.

The Second Secret is this: The golf swing is a swing. It's not a chop, a whack, a smack or a slam. It's a swing, and a swing feels easy-good-fun all at once. It's a swing, and it has an organic, natural feel—exactly the same feel as cutting grass or flinging the club toward the target. When you hit the ball, it's because the ball gets in the way of your swing. The ball is a minor encounter in the fullness of your swing. If you think of the golf swing like swinging on a playground swing set, hitting the ball is like scuffing the ground lightly with your feet when you swing through the bottom of the trajectory. If you think of your swing like cutting grass, hitting the ball is like trimming a millimeter off the top of the grass with your swing. If you think of your golf swing like driving your car around in a broad circle, hitting the ball is like running over a garden hose.

The Second Secret may sound obvious but it has a powerful lesson to teach us. The Second Secret says: Don't get so caught up in the goal of striking the ball that you forget that it's a swing. The great golfer Ken Venturi said it well: "Why are our practice swings the best swings? We don't think about the ball, only the flow." There are a lot of people in life who make themselves sick because they haven't mastered the Second Secret. They suffer from a variety of stress illnesses because they've lost touch with the flow. They don't know how to keep the easy-good-fun feeling alive in their bodies as they move through the stresses of everyday living.

I'll have more to say about all that a little further along. For now, though, let's keep our focus on golf.

A SECOND EXPERIMENT IN SWINGING

Pick up a club.

Have one in your hands? If not, you can use a substitute or just your arms.

Get some room around you, enough to swing the club around in various directions without hitting anybody or anything.

Close your eyes and keep them closed.

Relax with your eyes closed for a moment.

Make a commitment to enjoying life and being in the swing of things.

Begin to swing your body gently from side to side. Swing your weight gently from one leg to another. Make the transitions smooth and easy, as if your hip joints were on well-lubricated ball bearings.

Grip your club lightly and let it dangle in front of you.

Let the gentle swinging of your body inspire the club to swing gently back and forth.

Experiment with different speeds of swinging your body, and feel the club follow along with your changes in speed. Remember to keep your eyes closed.

Take your grip a little firmer, as if you were going to hit a ball. As you swing your body gently from side to side, begin to impart energy to the club with your wrists and arms.

Do this so that your body says, "Yes, this is a swing." Maybe you feel that right away; maybe it takes a while. Eventually your body will feel a swing.

When you feel a swing happening, deliberately grip your club tighter and change it to a chop or a slam. Make yourself try too hard on purpose. Feel the difference between swinging and trying too hard.

Then go back to a swing. Remember to keep your eyes closed. Do it all with your inner body awareness.

When you can feel a swing again, deliberately go to "not really being there." This is the opposite of trying too hard—it's not really giving a damn. Feel the difference between being in the swing of things and not really being there.

Then go back to swinging again. When you have your swing happening, open your eyes and continue to enjoy the feeling of swinging. When you get tired, wind down and take a rest. Activity and rest are part of the natural swing of life.

The Second Secret of the golf swing is that it feels easy-good-fun all at once. Ignoring or violating the Second Secret takes the fun out of golf. It takes the ease out of golf. It takes the good out of it. I see people out on the course all the time who don't have a clue about the Second Secret, and it doesn't look very attractive at all. Take the fun, the good and the ease out of a game and what do you have?

Fortunately the Second Secret can be learned quickly (though it takes a lifetime to master, on the course and off). All we have to do is ask ourselves three questions when we swing:

1. Is it easy?

2. Does it feel good?

3. Is it fun?

None of the answers can be faked, and you are the only judge that matters.

APPLYING THE SECOND SECRET TO BUSINESS AND LIFE

Understanding that the golf swing is a swing—not a chop, not a whack, not a swat—gives you a master key to successful golf. Even more important, it gives you a master key to success in business and life.

How does knowing "the swing is a swing" help you with business and life? First of all, a swing is free, easy and fun. Life and business can be that way, too. If the life we're living or the business we're doing doesn't feel free, easy and fun, we should probably take a close look at why it doesn't. I've learned from masters of business that it's possible to have a good time while doing very big things in the world. More than one of those masters have told me that the feeling of flow and ease is the main thing they keep an eye on in themselves. When the work—even the hard work and the long hours—stops feeling fun, they turn the bright searchlight of awareness on themselves and ask why.

Let's look more deeply into how the Second Secret—the swing is a swing—can help us in business and life. If you have a dictionary at hand, check out the definition of *swing*. My dictionary says that a swing is a "rhythmic movement back and forth."

Think of walking along in the spirit of a "rhythmic movement back and forth." You're in the swing of things. To be in the swing of things is to be moving along at the right pace in life. When you're not in the swing of things, it's usually because you're pushing yourself too hard or you're not engaged with the task at hand. Your attention is somewhere else.

Remember: Swinging feels good. It's easy and fun (unless you're going too fast or too high). That's an important thing to keep in mind: When things stop being easy and fun, it's often because we're pushing ourselves too fast, too hard or too high. It's time then to ease up, take a few breaths and get back into the swing.

By remembering that the golf swing is a swing, you remind yourself that it's supposed to feel good, easy and fun. If you're pushing yourself too hard, your swing won't feel like a swing. It'll feel like a chop, a whack, a swat or a slam. If you're not really there—if your attention is somewhere else—it will be a flail or a swish but it won't be a swing.

THE BIG SWING

There's an even bigger swing we all need to know about. It's our swing back and forth between forgetting and remembering that the whole game can feel free, easy and fun. In other words, the big swing—the meta-swing—is back and forth between losing the free and easy fun of life, then getting it back again.

I've gotten in the habit of asking myself frequently: Could this (whatever I'm doing) be even easier? Could this be more fun? At one point in my life, I realized it had been quite a while since I'd felt the free and easy feeling as I moved through my day. The fun had disappeared, and the game had become a grind. It took a lot of focused attention to get the fun and ease back. Nowadays, I ask myself frequently if I'm in the swing, because I don't want to lose it for as long.

Here's something to remember at every moment of golf, business and life: Forgetting and remembering are all part of the game. In golf, you swing back and forth between forgetting it's a swing and remembering it's a swing. I've done it countless times. I'll be out on the course, completely in the flow of ease, fun and good feeling. Then, some little circuit gets tripped in my brain and suddenly I'm trying too hard, taking it too seriously, growling at myself for a shanked shot. I'll go 'round and 'round in this loop for a while, then POP! I remember what it's all about. I chuckle, take an easy breath and remember that it's about fun, ease and good feeling.

In golf, you swing back and forth between forgetting it's fun and then remembering again. In business, you swing back and forth between getting lost in the stresses and dramas, then remembering it can be easy, fun and full of good feeling. In life, you swing back and forth between having a good time and then forgetting to have a good time. Then (hopefully) you remember again, and the good times roll.

In other words, forgetting is just as natural as remembering. You won't always be in the swing of things, nor will I. We swing back and forth. One moment we're having fun, swinging through life in an easeful flow, then CLUNK! For a while we feel clunky, off center and ill at ease. Then WHOOSH! We're back in the swing again. That's the way the game goes.

The Second Secret works miracles in the realm of relationships, both at home and at work. For example, both males and females swing back and forth between powerful needs for both closeness and independence. According to the great developmental psychologist

Margaret Mahler, our whole lives are defined by our swings back and forth between our needs for intimacy and our needs for individuation. When those two needs are in balance, we can enjoy our intimacy with others and our solitude with ourselves. Some of us ignore the pendulum swing of closeness and independence, preferring to swing only one way. Some of us immerse ourselves in the world of people, overlooking our individual development. Others of us shun our people needs, withdrawing to solo pursuits. When the swing is unswung or overswung, life gets out of balance.

The Second Secret makes your transitions easier and easier. Life itself is a swing back and forth between having a good time and not having a good time. The trouble is that many people get stuck on the not-having-a-good-time part of the swing. We often don't realize that it's within our own power to have a good time. We especially have a tough time learning that it's up to us to invent ways to get back to having a good time when we're stuck on not having a good time.

On the golf course, you might swing back and forth dozens of times between being in the swing and being out of the swing. On one tee you'll take an easy, harmonious swing and drive a beauty down the middle of the fairway. Then, on the very next tee you'll forget the feel of that easy swing. You'll grimace and take a heroic swat at the ball, trying to crush it into the next county. Instead of that mighty drive you were trying so hard to make, you'll hit a pathetic worm burner or slice it into the woods.

That's the way it goes. We go back and forth between fun and no-fun, flow and stuck, ease and tension. The important things to remember are it's a swing and you need to swing back to having a good time when you notice you're not.

If you absolutely can't find a way to get in the swing, take the hint and hang it up for the day. If your pendulum is jammed on the no-fun part of the swing, go home and lie down and come back another day. If you're not having a good time, you're not doing yourself or anybody else a favor by staying on the course.

I once gave an executive an unusual prescription, one that turned out to have an unexpected result. I was called in because he was driving his staff nuts by his moodiness. He would swing back and forth between exuberant elation and grumpy despair, sometimes two or three times a day. First, I arranged a medical workup with one of my colleagues. My client was around 50 years old, an age when many men have hormonal changes that can cause ups and downs. I gave him several coping strategies to use during the 3 days we had to wait for the lab results to get back. One of them was a simple breathing technique that quiets the body's stress chemistry within a couple of minutes. I told him to go in his office, put a DO NOT DISTURB sign on the door and do his breathing practice when he started feeling a grumpy mood coming on. I told him not to come out again until he had cleared the bad mood out of his body. He liked the breathing technique right away—he could feel the immediate difference when he did it—but he told me it was going to be hard to close himself off in the office, even for 2 minutes.

"Why?" I asked.

He looked at me as if the answer were obvious. "Because they need me," he said. "I'm indispensable."

That's when I knew he really needed to do it.

During the next 3 days he spent an average of an hour, all told, in his office doing his breathing. He learned that he could steady his moods with a simple breathing technique, but he also learned something of perhaps even greater value. His staff told him they had the most productive 3 days they could remember. The act of unplugging from his "indispensability" program gave them room to open up to more of their own creative energy. We also discovered that some of his male hormones had taken a midlife nosedive. Combining his breathing with hormonal supplementation, he was back on track in a few weeks.

WHOSE RULES ARE YOU PLAYING BY?

In business and life, there is no posted rule that says, "Life has to be hard." No company has a rule that says, "If you're not suffering, you're not really working." There's no duly elected authority figure or council that says, "Business has to be a struggle." I invite you to post your own rule that says, "Life and business are about having fun while inspiring others around me to have fun." Post a rule that says, "I can make more money having fun than I can by suffering."

A popular image of the successful businessperson is the hard-driving, table-pounding tyrant who terrorizes everybody around him or her. I've even met a few of them. But none of that is required. In fact, I know a few self-made billionaires. One of them is a quiet, easygoing fellow who wouldn't know how to pound on a table. I'm thinking of another one who's a fire-breathing table pounder. Now that I think about it, the easygoing guy got there first. He had a few billion in his thirties, whereas the other guy didn't get there until his fifties. The guy in his fifties probably had a lot less fun and a lot more stress along the way. Based on these two folks, I conclude that having a good time and being in the easy swing of things is financially rewarding as well as beneficial for our well-being.

The Second Secret suggests that we loosen our grip on the club so that it can be an easy swing. The swing is part holding on, part letting go. A successful businessman once told me something that I've used in my own life as well as in hundreds of coaching conversations. He said, "Some of the best deals I've ever done are the ones I didn't do." He said there had been many times when he would catch himself trying to force deals to come together. He would go home wiped out, after a day of stressing himself out with massive expenditures of energy. In his forties he wised up.

"If things require that much energy," he said, "I've learned to ask myself, 'Is this really what I should be doing?'" On more than one occasion he'd let go of a stressful deal, only to watch competitors go broke trying to put it together.

What a powerful insight! I immediately put it to work in my own life. I quickly found several areas where I'd been "pushing the river," with the usual meager success. Now, put the insight to work for you:

Where in your business life are you expending excess energy?

Most of us can identify a few areas where we're working overtime with little or no positive results. Identify a few of those areas of struggle, and then ask yourself:

"Should I be involved in that activity at all?"

Maybe you'll get a no, maybe a yes. If you get a no, look into how you might gracefully let go.

If you get a clear yes, ask yourself: "Could I do it with more ease? Could I keep the flow of good feeling while I do it?"

Even ask yourself a bolder question:

"Could I have fun doing it?"

Use the feeling of ease and fun in your body as a feedback mechanism that lets you know when you're on the right track. At first, the idea may seem ridiculous: Using ease and fun as ways of measuring your progress? Many people would argue that you're supposed to suffer, worry and feel anxious, and if you do enough of those you can go to bed satisfied that you've given your all to the day. Life is supposed to be hard, they might argue, and things like fun and ease should be regarded with suspicion. However, it's equally plausible that suffering and worry are the aberrations, and that life, business and golf are best navigated by using ease and fun as the compass settings.

Let's at least give ease, flow and fun a fair chance.

There is a simple way to find out in each moment whether we're in the flow, and a simple way to return to the flow when we've slipped out of it.

Give yourself 5 minutes now and then to master the following practice, and you may discover levels of ease and flow that have in the past seemed only fantasies.

YOUR 5-MINUTE DAILY PRACTICE FOR MASTERING THE SECOND SECRET

The simplest way to stay *in* the flow throughout your day is to stay *out* of fight-or-flight breathing. I begin my day—whether I'm at home or on the road—with a few minutes of the same breathing practice you're about to learn. It gets my flow going by getting my breathing centered, full and deep. Then, I return to it whenever I notice that the inevitable stresses of the day have knocked me off center into fight-or-flight breathing.

Fight-or-flight breathing means *chest breathing*. Centered breathing means *belly breathing*. When you respond to stress by getting anxious or angry, your breathing shifts into fight-or-flight mode. When you shift into fight-or-flight mode, your breathing gets shallower and faster and goes up into your chest. The muscles in your belly also get tight.

There have been thousands of scientific studies on the relationship of breathing and stress. It's a very complicated subject, but let me summarize simply the important thing we all need to know: When people become traumatized in some way—mentally, physically or emotionally—their breathing shows a specific trauma pattern. For example, if your father is yelling at you when you're a kid or if you slip and have a painful fall on a hard surface, your breathing will lock into a specific trauma pattern. This pattern can be seen throughout nature, in animals as well as humans.

Think of something like slipping and falling. One time in New England I stepped on a patch of ice and both feet shot out from under me. I slammed down on my tailbone, and it seemed to take months to stop hurting. Or think of receiving a reprimand from someone you fear—perhaps a cop who's just caught you for speeding.

When something like this happens, the trauma pattern kicks in: We suck in a sharp breath and hold it. When the feared object disappears, we let out the breath.

WHAT THE TRAUMA PATTERN IS ACTUALLY DOING

When the cop is chewing you out, you're trying to keep from getting emotional. You're trying to keep from bursting into tears, perhaps, or you're trying to keep from getting angry and defensive. The trauma pattern is to take in a breath and hold it, in order to help control your emotions. In physical trauma, it works the same way: We hold and restrict the breath to cut down on movement in the area that hurts. Once, I fell off my bike and whammed the right side of my rib cage on the pavement. For the next 3 weeks I felt a twinge of pain with every breath I took. Naturally, I took as tiny a breath as I possibly could—less movement, less pain.

The trauma pattern of breathing originated hundreds of thousands of years ago to help our animal ancestors keep still and unnoticed when in the presence of a feared object. If you're trying to hide from a saber-toothed tiger, it's to your advantage to hold your breath so your body won't move. So, please don't consider the trauma pattern a weakness or a moral failure—we truly wouldn't have gotten here without it.

The trick is simply to notice when you've shifted into traumatized breathing; the really big trick is knowing how to shift out of it.

Here's how.

The Instructions

(To help our worldwide community of clients, we've created moving animations and graphics on our Web site that show how to do this practice. The text instruction given here should be clear enough to get you started, but if you're a visual learner you may want to spend a few minutes watching the demonstrations at www.consciousgolf.biz).

The quickest way to awaken an easy feeling of flow in your body is to take a few belly breaths and flex your spine in a particular way. When we kick into fight-or-flight breathing, our breath goes up into our chest, our bellies tighten and our spines stiffen. Don't take it personally—it's the way all mammals handle stress. We tighten, stiffen and pump ourselves up with adrenaline by chest breathing. Common sense tells us that to shift out of stress we need to relax our bellies, flex our spines and let our breathing drop out of the chest and back into the belly. That's what this practice does. It's very efficient, too. Just a few breaths will get you out of the off-center feeling of stress and back into the flow.

Here's how to flex your spine for maximum flow. Remember, you have to do this only a few times to get the flow feeling going. I do it first thing in the morning for a few minutes, and can't imagine life without it.

Sitting toward the front of a chair (so that your back has room to move), rock slowly front to back on your sit bones. Take several seconds to rock to the front slowly, then take several seconds to rock back. As you rock toward the front, notice that your head naturally wants to tilt upward. When you rock back toward your tail bone, your head naturally wants to tilt downward.

Rock your pelvis toward the front while tilting your head upward toward the ceiling. Then rock your pelvis backward, tilting your chin toward the floor. Do this movement over and over, but keep it gentle, easy and comfortable.

When you're comfortable with this movement, add your breathing to it. As you rock your pelvis forward and tilt your chin up, take a full, deep breath into your relaxed belly. Let the breath expand your belly completely. As you rock your pelvis backward, breathe all the way out slowly.

Continue this easy, gentle breath-movement for a couple of minutes. When I'm home, I do it for a few minutes in the morning, sitting on one of those big inflatable gymnastic balls. When I'm on the road, I sit on the edge of the bed or a chair in my hotel room. Wherever I am, my goal is the same: to get a pleasant, easeful flow of energy going in my body. I've found that if I devote a few minutes to this practice first thing in the morning, I can return to the flow easily throughout the day when I get knocked off center. If I skip the morning practice, it takes longer to get centered later in the day when I encounter the inevitable stresses.

The Golf Version

For golfers, I also recommend a few minutes of the practice in the morning. We've developed a specific set of instructions for using your breathing to your advantage on the course.

Good golfers do something different with their breathing—something you may not know how to do. I want to show you what it is, because it will not only make you a better golfer but it will also help you remember the First Secret when you're on the course.

When I got interested in golf, I began watching videos of the best golfers to discover if they were breathing differently when they hit the ball. I made an astounding discovery—there it was, plain as day. Top golfers routinely breathed in an entirely different way from not-so-top golfers. Once I saw what it was, I immediately put it to use. Then I realized something even more profound. The breath secret of top golfers relates directly to our First Secret! In other words, *superb golfers apply the First Secret to their breathing*! From talking to top golfers, I found that almost all of them do this breath secret totally unconsciously. Somehow they learned (or were perhaps born with the knowledge) that this particular way of breathing makes them hit a better shot.

Overcoming Fear

From interviewing amateur golfers, I've discovered several fears that grip them when they go to hit a golf ball. One is the fear of looking stupid. It's a fear of doing something that gets a snicker from a real or imaginary onlooker. I believe this fear is related to having been shamed or criticized in childhood.

A second fear is the actual physical fear of striking the ground. I believe this fear relates to prior traumas in which the person actually struck the ground through slips, falls and other unpleasant encounters with solid objects.

Regardless of the specific fear, the golfer sucks in a breath and often holds it before or during the golf swing. In other words, the unskilled golfer *tries to hit while activating the trauma reflex*! In reviewing videos of professional golfers, I've found that they almost never do this.

The skilled golfer swings during an out-breath or just after an out-breath. In other words, they make the effort, which is the golf swing, in exactly the way nature has designed it to be done—with an out-breath. Watch a weight lifter sometime on TV. You'll never, ever see one breathe in as he or she performs the exertion. That's because nature has wired us so that we perform effort best on the out-breath or just after an out-breath. With weight lifters, you can usually hear their out-breath, in the form of a grunt or similar out-breath sound. You can even see this same pattern in sports with lesser exertion such as tennis. Many tennis players grunt or make exclamations as they strike the ball.

Here's how that relates to the First Secret. The out-breath signifies completion. Obviously, a complete breath is made up of an in and an out. If we try to hit the ball while breathing in, we're trying to hit in a state of incompletion. If we hit the ball while breathing out—or just after breathing out, as good golfers tend to do—we're taking advantage of nature's organic pattern of completion.

The 2-Minute Experiment

Take a few swings while breathing in. In other words, do it backward from the way good golfers do it. Discover how it feels to breathe "wrong" when you swing.

Now take a few swings while you're breathing out. Make your swing in coordination with the flow of breath out of your nose. Feel the difference between this swing and the in-breath swing you tried first.

Now take a few more swings after you've completed an out-breath. Let the breath all the way out and take your swing during the still point after the out-breath.

Repeat this sequence over and over for a couple of minutes. Do an in-breath swing, followed by an out-breath swing. Then do a swing after the end of the out-breath.

I discovered that I make a cleaner ball strike if I take a full out-breath, then swing. Everybody is a little different, though, so I encourage you to experiment to find the right way for you.

On the Course of Life
and in the Course of the Business Day

Apply this practice as you move through your day. Notice your breathing as you go through the key activities of living. Notice particularly when you hold your breath and when your breath shifts up into your chest. This will show you what scares you. From the reports of people I've worked with—as well as from my own observations—I predict that you'll be amazed at the number of times your breathing will shift into fight-or-flight mode during the course of life.

Notice also when your breathing feels full and deep

and nurturing. This will show you when you're participating fully in the flow of life. Ideally, we would feel an easy flow of life energy all the time. Until we master this elusive state, the best we can do is to discover what triggers us to fight and flee, and to return to the flow of full participation as often as we can.

"No problem can
be solved from the same
consciousness that
created it."

—ALBERT EINSTEIN

CHAPTER 4

THE ULTIMATE SECRET

I've saved the greatest of all secrets for last. When you hear it, you may think it sounds incredibly simple. It is. However, this secret has truly vast implications for every moment of our lives. Understand its deep wisdom and you cannot fail to enjoy golf, business and life with more zest. And though the secret is utterly obvious, the implications of it have been hidden in plain sight. It's been so carefully concealed by our programming that many people go to their graves without catching a glimpse of it. Once you see it, you'll never be the same. I've actually seen grown-ups in my seminars stagger around laughing hysterically as the implications sunk in.

Ready? Here goes.

When you hit a golf ball, you're in motion. The ball is not.

The ball doesn't go anywhere until you hit it.

It just sits there until you put the energy into it.

The ball is just a ball, and it's going to stay put until you strike it.

However it spins and wherever it goes, you're the one who put the spin on it. You're the one who sent it wherever it went.

Once again: The ball sits there. We deliver the energy it needs to go where it's going to go.

In golf, we bring everything to the ball. In business and life, we bring all the meaning to each moment. The moment sits there. We charge it with action and meaning.

That's why golf is the greatest of all games, right up there with business and life. It's why you can learn everything you really need to learn about life on the course. It's also why you can see grown-ups doing very immature things out there on the course. I played at a course a few times where a fellow had gone bonkers after a "bad" shot and had beaten most of the bark off a tree. He beat on the tree until he destroyed his driver, then got another club out of his bag and chopped some more wood. I heard that he was a mild-mannered insurance executive in real life. Something happened that day that turned him into an amateur lumberjack and got him banished from the club for life.

Although I wasn't there, I can guess what happened: He had an encounter with the Third Secret. More to the point, he came up against the big problem in life, and he didn't know the Third Secret—the secret that could have solved his problem, and the wood could have been spared.

Let's walk through what must have happened that day.

Our insurance man hit the ball, and it did not go where he thought it should have gone. It was probably not the first time it happened that day.

At moments like these, the conscious golfer thinks, "Hmmm, what did I do that caused the ball to go where it went?" The conscious golfer looks at reality and concludes, "Regardless of my hopes, dreams and expectations, the ball landed exactly where it should have landed."

The unconscious golfer thinks, "It is unacceptable that the ball could be where it apparently is. The physical universe is wrong, and I must punish it."

He fixes upon a nearby representative of the physical universe—in this case a tree—and he begins to beat on it with a club. However, in the war between us and the world, says the late Frank Zappa, "back the world." The tree is still standing (though slightly chewed up), but the golfer is long gone.

The big problem of life stares you right in the face with every golf shot. The ball is just sitting there until you put your spin on it—just like life.

Someone may have told you that life is hard. They were wrong. Someone may have told you that life is beautiful. They were wrong, too. The truth is: Life isn't *anything* until we *is* it. It's up to us to put the *is* in life. Nobody can truthfully say, "Life is beautiful" or "Life is awful," because these are simply interpretations. Two different people could apply completely different interpretations to the same event.

"I had a flat tire once in the middle of a busy downtown street," says Jack.

"How awful," says Jim, plastering his own meaning all over Jack's flat tire.

"No, it was actually the most beautiful experience of my life," says Jack. "Otherwise, I would never have met my wife, the tow-truck driver."

If you try to apply your interpretation across the board—in other words, if you think your interpretation and reality are the same thing—you can actually put yourself in danger. Try saying to somebody who's in a bad mood, "Hey! Lighten up! Life is actually beautiful." You just might get your sniffer bent in a new direction. The person in a bad mood is putting a different spin on life at that moment. If you step in and try to spin the person in the other direction, look out! If you want to attempt such a meaning-implant, be very careful of your timing and your context. From 30 years of therapy experience, I can tell you that you have to be careful even when people are paying you to help them with the bad mood. All good therapists learn a simple trick early in their careers, which is to acknowledge the way people are spinning before trying to spin them in another direction. Instead of saying, "Lighten up—life is beautiful," good therapists learn to say things like "You're in a bad mood—let's take a moment to feel and honor that experience. Then, let's find out how you got that way."

GOLF REALLY STICKS IT TO US

Golf really sticks one of life's big problems right in our faces. Other games are easier on us. For example, if you swing at a baseball and miss, you can always blame it on the quality of the pitch. The pitcher "got one by you." Maybe he "fooled you" or "threw you a curveball." God forbid, maybe the pitch was so good that you "got caught looking." In baseball and most other sports, you always have something or someone to blame—if all else fails, both sides can attain momentary unity by blaming the umpire or referee.

Golf solves that little problem in a maddeningly ingenious way—by giving us a big stick to swing and a little ball that just sits there. With this brilliant flash of simplicity, golf gives us a chance to solve the biggest problem that lurks in our psyches: projection. From Beverly Hills to Belfast to Beirut, projection causes immense trouble in our personal and political worlds.

Projection is when you point at something *out there* and think it's responsible for something inside you. When projection is extreme, it's laughably obvious. When it's found lurking in ourselves, it's not so obvious and we don't usually think it's so funny. Once, early in my training as a psychologist, I had occasion to learn about projection from a man who had lived in a mental hospital for quite a while. He was afraid to leave the grounds because the space aliens who inhabited the telephone wires controlled his moods and his actions.

That's what I mean when I say projection is sometimes laughably obvious. I actually thought he was joking when he said it, but the tables would soon turn on me and my naivete. I lobbed a joking reply back to him: "The aliens aren't in those phone lines anymore—they all moved to the countryside where they still use copper lines. They can't stand the plastic in those new fiber optics."

He chuckled ruefully and shook his head. "That's where you're a little off-track, young fellow. That's what they *want* you to think."

WHERE MISERY COMES FROM

We humans have perfected the art of making ourselves miserable, and the main way we do it is with projection. In a movie theater, we don't pay attention to the projector because it's behind us. The actual source of the pictures is behind us, but the pictures show up on the wall in front of us. The audience tends to forget this cunning trick. We get lost in the story, so we think it's actually happening up there on the wall we're staring at.

When I was a kid growing up in the South, I often went to Saturday afternoon matinees. Kids could get in for a dime; our parents probably thought it was the greatest child-care bargain ever invented. We were not a sophisticated audience. In fact, we were a bunch of scruffy swamp rats in a backwater town in central Florida. During those great films like *Godzilla* and *Creature from the Black Lagoon*, I have actually seen kids stand up and start yelling at the screen. Often it was a warning, "LOOK OUT! THERE'S A MONSTER IN THE CLOSET!"

We all have this problem to some degree. We forget that we're the source of how we see the world. The moment we forget that, we start thinking that the world actually is a certain way. We forget that we're the ones running the projector and shining the light. It looks like life is happening "over there." In life, we forget that we are projecting our reality onto everything we experience. We forget that we're making up the way we see the world based on our own needs and past experiences.

We also forget that we're making up how we see other people. As we slide deeper into projection, we start thinking other people actually *are* a certain way. We sink into the trance a little deeper and think life itself *is* a certain way. We even go so far as to *argue* that it's a certain way. We go around saying things like "Life is hard" and "You can't trust people." It's much rarer to hear someone say, "I've created a hard life for myself" or "I've trusted people indiscriminately and felt disappointed."

Let me give you a very practical business example to show why this point is so important. See if you can relate to my client Philip. I certainly found a lot of myself in him.

Philip sold real estate. He came in for a session to work on a specific pattern that he wanted to break. Specifically, he had been stuck at an income ceiling of $70,000 a year for the past 5 years. What brought him to me was a maddening occurrence the previous year. He had made $100,000 (and even bought a bottle of expensive champagne to celebrate breaking through his ceiling). However, almost before the bubbles had fizzed, his breakthrough had fizzled. A tax anomaly came out of left field, and when the chips had been counted he ended the year slightly under $70,000 again.

What makes Philip different from a lot of us is that he realized he had a repetitive pattern going. Many of us have patterns that repeat—we just don't realize they're patterns. We think it's just how life is and has to be. Indeed, Philip had never seen the pattern until his new wife, who had taken a class of mine at the

University of Colorado, heard the story and insisted he see me.

Philip came in so wide-open to learning that he had his breakthrough at breakneck speed. It emerged that his father also sold real estate. I asked: "How much does your father typically earn selling real estate?" Philip didn't know, but he told me his father was only modestly successful. In fact, he expressed sadness that his father had grown bitter in his sunset years because he'd never really "made it." A light began to dawn in my mind. "Let's get your father on the phone," I said.

Philip agreed, and we soon had Dad on the phone. I explained who I was and what Philip was up to. I didn't mention any numbers, though, until I popped the following question: "If you don't mind my asking, what's the maximum you've earned in any 1 year?"

You can probably guess the amount. It was $70,000.

How does something like this happen? Philip swore up and down that he had no actual knowledge of his father's ceiling, nor had he ever discussed his own ceiling with his father. How do such things get transmitted from one person to the other?

It's a mystery to me, then and now. However, it's

not important to know why—what's important is that Philip put the information to work. I took him through a procedure I use that helps people change the unconscious limitations they've imposed on themselves. The process reveals the emotional underpinning of the issue. In Philip's case, the emotion that lay at the bottom of the issue was an overidentification with his father's grief. The father had never really recovered from the death of his wife, Philip's mother, when Philip was a teenager. Philip had taken care of his father during this time, and as a result Philip had never fully completed his own grieving process. Father and son had unconsciously become brothers in grief, and this bond had caused Philip to decide never to go beyond his father, lest his father feel left behind again.

Philip doubled his income the following year. The pattern was broken, and perhaps more important, the bond with his father became even stronger because it was now based on clarity and love rather than undigested grief.

That's the Third Secret at work.

It all comes down to realizing that we are in motion; the ball isn't. It's not the ball—it's us. It's not the ceiling of $70,000 that's real—it's our frozen-up meaning-machinery that creates the limitation. We absolutely have to realize this if we're going to have a shot at big-time success and big-time happiness. We have to realize that until we get the Third Secret deeply embodied within us, we're at the mercy of chance when we could be at choice.

There's a cartoon that shows three panhandlers making signs for their fund-raising efforts. Two of the panhandlers are experienced and one is a novice. The two experienced guys are making signs that say things like "I'm a victim of society" and "I had a terrible childhood." The new guy's sign says: "I got here through a succession of poor choices." The first two are shaking their heads and telling him, "You're not going to make a nickel that way."

It's often painful to accept that we got where we are through a succession of choices, but that's the only perspective that has any real power to it. Thinking as a victim hands all the power over to others—all we get in return is a lifetime ticket to complain and some sympathy, if we're lucky.

In golf, everybody knows deep inside that there's nothing we can blame our misfortunes on. That's why angry eruptions look so tacky and out of place on a golf course. Believe it or not, I've actually seen golfers hit a shot they didn't like and blame it on the ball. "Bad ball!" I've seen others blame it on the course. "This stupid course!" Others get angry at their clubs, their fellow players and sometimes God. Some, of course, blame it on themselves, which is just as big a mistake as blaming it on God. Blame always looks tacky and out of place on the course, for one good reason.

There's nobody to blame. Not even ourselves.

In golf and life and everything else, there's never anything to blame. *There's always only something to learn.* From each moment of golf, from each moment of life, we have something we can learn.

That's why there's no such thing as a bad shot. Never.

You cannot make a bad golf shot.

You can hit a shot and *think* it's bad, but who brought the concept of "bad" to the shot?

The shot always goes exactly where it's supposed to go. The upset comes because we think it was supposed to go somewhere else. But where did the concept of "somewhere else" come from?

The Third Secret gives us the chance of a lifetime in every moment. In every moment we have the opportunity to be in relationship with whatever is occurring. If we are fully in relationship with the ball, for example, we'll want to know where it goes and how it got there. If we are truly in relationship with the ball, we won't want to impose our notions of where it should go onto it. We should come into such an intimate relationship with the ball that it becomes our teacher, our guru, our best friend. The very best teacher teaches us to know what is real. In Sanskrit, the word *guru* means "one who dispels illusion." Our best friends are those who will point out reality to us, as gently or forcefully as the situation requires. That's why I say that the ball is your best friend. It always gives you immediate feedback on exactly what you did that made it go where it went. Whether the ball gives its feedback gently or forcefully depends entirely on how open or resistant we are to learning at the moment we see where it lands.

The Third Secret frees us from projecting our illusions onto reality. It teaches us reverence for the real, respect for the way things are. If I hit the ball and it veers off into the rough, I can remain at peace by applying the Third Secret. "Hmmm," I think to myself, "my body must have had an intention to hit it over there into the rough. My conscious intention may have been to hit a beautiful shot, but my conscious mind obviously didn't get informed about my intention to hit the ball into the rough. The results, however, always show me what my true intention is."

Unwise golfers, those who are ignorant of the Third Secret, make themselves miserable by dividing themselves in two. They erroneously think there is a "good" part of them who had an intention to hit a beautiful shot, and a "mistaken" part of them that goofed up and hit the shot into the rough. I counsel my clients (and myself) to do away with this artificial division—especially because it doesn't exist, anyway. Assume that your results tell you what your intentions are, and you'll never waste another precious learning-moment thinking "I didn't mean to do *that*."

PRACTICALLY SPEAKING

Some of our biggest upsets come when we project our expectations onto the moment. One way to make ourselves instantly miserable is to hover over each moment in a state of expectation. When the moment doesn't occur according to our expectation, here comes the freight train, hauling a load of upset. We're standing on the tracks, caught up in the fantasy world of our expectation, when WHOMP! The freight train wins every time.

Expectation can really take the fun out of golf. It can

take the fun out of every tick of the second hand, all day long. When I was first married, I had a habit of listening with a certain set of expectations when my wife talked to me about certain subjects. For example, my wife might be telling me about her feelings, saying she was tired or unhappy about something. As she spoke, I'd be listening with the expectation that she wanted me to fix whatever problem she had. In other words, I'd be "listening-to-fix." It's a kind of listening filter, one that alters the content of the message coming in. If she was telling me about being angry with our son, I'd be busily trying to figure out what she could do to keep from being angry. If she was telling me she was tired, I'd be busy thinking up ways she could feel more rested.

Finally one day she said, "Hey, would you just listen instead of offering advice? I'm capable of fixing myself—all I want you to do is listen. I'm telling you these things so you'll know what's going on inside me, not because I need you to figure out some solution." At first I couldn't understand this concept—"You mean you just want me to listen and resonate with you? You mean I'm not supposed to do anything to fix it?"

That was a big day around the house, I can tell you. I realized I'd been doing this kind of filtered listening all my life. It was a habit I'd learned in my family. They were great critics of others and veritable fountainheads of advice. (This was especially true if the people were not themselves. They weren't quite so skillful when it came to fixing their own addictions or actually following their own advice!) In fact, now that I have more life experience, I think I've figured out what they were trying to do. They focused on criticizing and fixing other people to avoid the pain of acknowledging that they had no idea how to fix themselves. I know about this because I woke up one day and realized I was doing it myself.

I discovered that I listened with expectations a good bit of the time. By observing myself and by asking for feedback from my wife and others, I discovered I had other listening filters, such as "listening-to-find-fault" and "listening-to-rebut." I gradually let go of those filters and haven't missed them at all. Now, I do my best to practice "just listening." I think of "just" as having a double meaning. It's just listening in the sense of pure listening with nothing else added. It's also just listening in the sense of justice. When something is just, it is true, accurate and fair. That's what I'm aiming for in my listening now.

Most of the expectations we haul around with us are unnecessary. Some are useful; most are not—it's up to us to find out which are which. I'll give you an example of one that's not worth keeping. I'm not a natural athlete. My grandfather, who raised me, was an incredible natural athlete. When he was 75 years old he could outrun people half his age. He must have spent hundreds of frustrating hours trying to show me how to hit a baseball, how to hit a tennis ball, how to hit anything. I just never seemed to get it. I developed the impression that I wasn't good at sports, and my various attempts did nothing to budge this impression. I was okay at football in high school, but mainly because I was big. My coach made me a defensive lineman because he astutely saw that even if I did nothing but flop down in a heap on each play, I would at least provide a large mound of obstruction to get around. I remember him telling me over and over, "Don't do anything—just fall down!" Even then, I was no more than mediocre.

One day years later, I caught myself in the grip of this old expectation. On the golf course, I realized I was hovering over the ball with the expectation that I wasn't going to hit a good shot—*because I wasn't good at sports*. My expectation had gotten there before I did. I took a deep breath and let this realization wash over me.

I realized the truth of the matter—the notion that I wasn't good at sports had absolutely nothing to do with whether I hit the golf ball or not. If you put a hundred natural athletes on the course against a hundred unnatural athletes, the natural athletes would probably turn in better scores, but *so what*?

I decided to make up a new reality, that I could hit fine golf shots regardless of whether I had ever been any good at sports. I tossed out my old reality and haven't missed it a bit. When I get up on the tee box I just hit the golf ball, regardless of whether I'm "good at sports." As you might imagine, I hit it a lot better.

You can do that, too.

You probably will want to keep some of your expectations—especially the ones that are keeping you safe and sound.

Here's one I decided was worth keeping:

I've never had an auto accident in 40 years of driving. I give credit to a type of expectation that hovers in the background when I drive. I've avoided a number of accidents by assuming the other driver was going to do the stupidest possible thing, then making sure I wouldn't be affected by it. In one situation, a person who'd had his right blinker on for two blocks suddenly decided to turn left. I'd been tempted to pass him on the left—nobody was coming and it was the logical thing to do. Something in his manner, though, inspired me to apply my stupidest-possible-thing rule, and I'm glad I did. Another time, I noticed one of those all-terrain three-wheel motorcycles bouncing around in the back of a pickup truck flying down the freeway a couple of hundred feet ahead. I pointed it out to my wife, who was driving at the time. I wondered out loud if the driver had been stupid enough not to tie down his three-wheeler. I wondered whether he was so oblivious that he wasn't noticing it bouncing a lot as he roared along at 80 miles per hour.

He turned out to be just that oblivious. My wife slowed up, then moved over into another lane. We decided to pull up beside him and point at the loose three-wheeler. We never got to do that, though, because he hit a bump and the three-wheeler flew out of the truck and crashed onto the road with a mighty spray of sparks. When last we saw it, it was bouncing down the freeway end over end. I'm firmly convinced that my drivers-will-often-do-the-stupidest-possible-thing expectation may have saved our lives.

However, if I had the expectation that friends and

family should be treated to the same vigilance, lest they do the stupidest-possible thing, I probably wouldn't be much fun to be around. Imagine how unpleasant it would be if I were sipping a glass of Château Lafite Rothschild at dinner in a wonderful restaurant with my wonderful wife, while expecting her to say the stupidest-possible thing. I've seen couples who seemed to be dining that way, and it didn't look like they were enjoying their meals.

Most of our expectations are not useful in any way. If we hover over each moment in a state of expectation, we're not really present to what's actually happening. In golf, the less expectation the better. Only the moment matters.

There is the ball, which is utterly at rest until we hit it.

There is the swing, which is charged with our energy, personality and intention.

There is the ultimate completion of the moment, the interface when club face meets ball. The shot flies off to its destiny, as awful or sublime as we wish to make it. If we have learned to greet reality with a loving embrace, every shot is sublime because we can learn something from where it goes. If we cringe against reality with a clenched jaw and a closed mind, we will find fault with every shot except a hole in one.

I once enjoyed the rare treat of playing golf with one of my boyhood heroes, Chicago Cubs shortstop Ernie Banks. At breakfast before our round of golf, I asked Ernie to tell me who was the toughest pitcher he ever faced. I expected him to say either Bob Gibson or Sandy Koufax, but his answer surprised and delighted me. He told me he never paid the slightest attention to who the pitcher was. "My job was to hit the ball—it didn't matter who was throwing it."

No expectation! And no wonder he had such success hitting the ball. He wasn't hovering over the ball thinking "Koufax has great stuff today" or "Gibson has his 95-mile-an-hour fastball going." There was only the ball, and his job was to hit it.

We can all benefit from Ernie's tip, whether we're playing golf, doing business or living life. No moment of golf, business or life requires expectation on our part. If we think we should have swung another way or think the ball should have gone to another place, we are missing the key point: We took our swing, and the ball went where it went.

If we get the point here, we get it everywhere.

Why? Because golf is life.

Because there is only one game and we're playing it all the time.

Because there is only one life, and *this is it*!

PRACTICE SESSION

Putting the Ultimate Secret into Play

APPLYING THE ULTIMATE SECRET TO BUSINESS AND LIFE

Now we come to our final practice, one that can add value to every moment of our existence. In golf, business and life, there is a specific intention that makes all of those games a total blast. When you approach golf, business and life from one specific intention, you can enjoy being in a sand trap or a traffic jam as much as cashing a check for $1 million. With one specific intention you can have a great time all the time.

The intention: to learn from every interaction.

When we're open to learning in every situation, we can move very quickly through the rough spots. The reason: We get the message quicker about how we got into those spots. In my own life, as well as in coaching thousands of people, I've found that there is an exhilaratingly clear correlation between success and openness to learning. Incredibly successful people are incredibly open to learning. My experience has shown me that forming the intention to learn from every moment of life changes every moment of life for the better.

Contrast this intention with a more typical one: the intention to judge every interaction. This intention requires us to inspect every moment and judge it right or wrong, good or bad, perfect or not. Letting go of this intention is one of the best things any human being can do.

YOUR 5-MINUTE DAILY PRACTICE FOR MASTERING THE ULTIMATE SECRET

The Business Practice

In the beginning I recommend doing this practice for a few minutes. Later, you may find you can get the same results in a few seconds.

In the quiet of your own mind, try on the following commitment:

"I commit to learning something new from every interaction I have today."

Repeat it several times until you have the meaning of it clearly established.

When the meaning of it is clear, repeat it several

more times, pausing between each mental repetition to feel it in your body. Grade yourself only on sincerity. Each time you try it on in your body, evaluate whether you sincerely commit to learning something new from every interaction.

Understanding the Commitment

Learning is about discovering something new. It's not about confirming something you knew already. For example, let's say you already think Fred is a jerk. If you have an interaction with Fred today and come away thinking "Fred is a jerk," you really haven't learned anything. However, if in your interaction you discovered a better way of relating to him so that his being a jerk didn't cause any inconvenience, you've learned something from the interaction.

Learning is not about judging or being right or confirming your suspicions. Learning is about discovery. When you make a commitment to learning from every interaction, you're committing to a lifelong, moment-by-moment process of discovery. That's big fun. I haven't had a dull moment in the past 30 years since I figured out this little secret.

The secret can be applied to every moment of existence. Each moment can be greeted with the attitude of "Hmmm, what can I learn from this?" For pure, nonstop fun in every moment, I'll put this attitude up against any other one I've ever heard about.

Contrast the attitude of "learning from every moment" to other popular attitudes. One popular attitude I see in business is "finding fault with everything that occurs." Another attitude is "How busy can I look without actually accomplishing anything?"

Take a few moments each morning to reawaken a commitment to learning from every interaction throughout the day. You'll see that it makes the ever-changing environment of modern business a much saner place. If we greet each moment of change with "Hmmm, what do I need to learn here?" we can dance with the very same changes we might otherwise find ourselves grappling with.

The Golf Practice

The same wisdom applies to the game of golf. Many players on the course greet every shot with a judgmental attitude. I hear so many negative, judgmental comments on the golf course! Just listen next time you're out there on the course. Notice what happens when someone says, "Good shot." Often the player receiving the compliment will respond with a judgment instead of a simple "Thanks." The judgment will be something like "Naaa, I topped it a little" or "If I'd hit it a little lower, the wind wouldn't have caught it." It's very rare for somebody to respond with a pure, unadorned "Thanks." Rarer still to hear someone respond with a clear learning attitude: "Hmmm, what did I do that made it go there?"

Instructions

Place a ball on the floor or on the ground. Select a target for your putt.

Take your putter in hand and address the ball.

Before you strike the ball, pause for a moment and make an inner commitment to this effect:

I commit to learning from where this ball goes when I putt it. I specifically release any commitment to judging this putt as good or bad.

Now, putt the ball.

The moment it comes to rest, say the following sentence in your mind: "Hmmm, what did I do that caused it to go there?"

As soon as you say this sentence in your mind, shift

your attention to your body and feel what you did that made the ball go where it went.

Repeat the sequence with a number of putts.

Address the ball, and make the commitment to learn instead of judge.

Then, make your putt. When the ball rolls to a stop, repeat your "Hmmm . . ." sentence in your mind. Then, feel in your body what you did that made the ball go wherever it went.

On the Course of Life

Notice how much of your attention goes into judging things as right or wrong, good or bad, smart or stupid, perfect or not. When I first began this practice, I discovered to my horror that I judged a great deal more than I thought I did. I fancied myself an easygoing and tolerant person; *judgmental* would have been one of the last adjectives I would have used to describe myself. As I observed more closely, though, I found that my judging was simply more subtle and covert than I had realized. When I quit judging myself for being judgmental, my life took a quantum shift toward more success and enjoyment.

Here's to learning from every moment, now into infinity, and to the infinite joy that comes from learning.

CHAPTER 5

THE FAIRWAY: A FAREWELL BLESSING

The meaning I've chosen for life can be summarized in a few simple sentences:

• We are deeply fortunate to be here at all—
this life is a gift to cherish in every moment.

• It's up to us to have a good time
while we're here.

• We can have the very best time
by helping others have a great time.

Everything else is frosting on the cake. Thousands of species have come and gone from the earth, and we could be next on the list for immediate extinction. So let's celebrate the great gift of life by enjoying ourselves immensely while assisting others in enjoying themselves.

If we should find ourselves on this fine planet and on a golf course, too, we are blessed beyond all imagining. How amazing that this universe could create this earth! How remarkable that this earth could create this life! How splendidly improbable that this life could have created me! That I should find myself sitting quietly, pen in hand and golf clubs at my side, overlooking a gorgeous expanse of green, with the blue Pacific in the background—well, that's a miracle beyond all reckoning.

It's an infinite fairway of blessings, pure and simple.

And now, let me extend those blessings to you. May the moments of your life be abundant and deeply savored. May you roam through endless beauty with wonderful companions. May you swing with equal joy on the fairway and in the rough. May you cherish the miracle of every step as you walk the full round of your life.

If our paths should cross someday, and I truly hope they will, let's greet each other in the spirit of celebration. Until we meet again, let's walk in magnificent completion through our world, making every step the fair way by virtue of how we stride.

Thank you for letting me speak my mind and heart with you.